WALKING PEPYS'S LONDON

About the Author

Jacky Colliss Harvey worked in museum publishing for many years and as a writer and commentator on the arts and their relationship to popular culture. She is the author of the *New York Times* bestseller *RED: A History of the Redhead* and *The Animal's Companion: People and their Pets, a 26,000-Year-Old Love Story*. A country mouse by birth, she has been fascinated by London and its multifarious history since first arriving in the city as a student.

Walking Pepys's London

Jacky Colliss Harvey

Published in Great Britain in 2021 by
The Armchair Traveller (an imprint of Haus Publishing Ltd)
4 Cinnamon Row, London SW11 3TW

www.hauspublishing.com
@HausPublishing

Cartography produced by ML Design
Maps contain OS data © Crown Copyright and database right (2020)

A CIP catalogue for this book is available from the British Library

ISBN: 978-1-909961-82-1
eISBN: 978-1-913368-29-6

Typeset in Garamond by MacGuru Ltd
Printed in the United Kingdom

This one is for my Twin, with love and gratitude.
T'Other Twin

Contents

Introduction   1
Author's Note   15

Walk 1: From Westminster to the City   17
Walk 2: Through the City to Seething Lane   45
Walk 3: A Night Out with Mr Pepys   69
Walk 4: Along the River to Greenwich   95
Walk 5: A New Year's Day Walk   123

Acknowledgements   145
Bibliography   147
Index   149
Digital Walking Routes   157

Introduction

SAMUEL PEPYS, walker, accidental historian, and creator of the most celebrated diary in English literature, was born in a house at the Fleet Street end of Salisbury Court, London, EC4Y 8AA on 23 February 1633 – making him, for those with an interest in such matters, a Pisces and his celestial ruler Neptune.

Salisbury Court (now complete with a blue plaque to commemorate its most famous son) is an alleyway that runs pretty much straight north to south; its other end, in Pepys's day, dipped down into the Thames at the landing stage of Dorset Stairs. The area took its name from Salisbury House, a hostelry of the grandest sort, built on land originally owned by the Bishop of Salisbury and notable for lodging, among others, Prince Arthur in 1498. By Pepys's time, Salisbury House had become Dorset House, the London seat of the Sackvilles. From 1629, Salisbury Court was also home to Salisbury Court Theatre. You might say that Pepys, the archetypal Londoner, was from his first breath encircled by all the elements – social, cultural, architectural, and topographical – that formed the city that was to make his fortune and his name; and, as the future Chief Secretary to the Admiralty, that he had a goodly splash of aquatic pre-destination thrown in.

The aim of this book is to acquaint the reader with London as it was lived in Pepys's day from the pavement up, and as her streets were experienced by Pepys himself. Pepys was a prodigious walker. The two-and-a-half miles to Whitehall from his house in Seething Lane were accomplished on an almost daily basis, and so many of his professional conversations took place while walking with a confidante or patron that the streets became for him an alternative to his office. But Pepys didn't only walk his city, he observed it: its daily face, its other inhabitants, the systems that kept it functioning, the new powers within it replacing the old. And his recording of these observations in his famous diary not only gives us an unparalleled means of time-travelling back more than 350 years but also makes Pepys a sort of seventeenth-century London version of the celebrated nineteenth-century Parisian *flâneur*: the 'passionate observer', one whose greatest enjoyment was to 'establish his dwelling in the throng, in the ebb and flow, the bustle', the man for whom, as Baudelaire put it, 'The crowd is his domain'. Pepys walked because he liked to walk. 'Young Michell [the son of one of Sam's regular booksellers] and I, it being an excellent frosty day to walk, did walk out,' he writes on 6 January 1667,

> he showing me the baker's house in Pudding Lane, where
> the late great fire begun; and thence all along Thames Street,
> where I did view several places, and so up by London Wall, by
> Blackfriars, to Ludgate; and thence to Bridewell, which I find
> to have been heretofore an extraordinary good house, and a fine
> coming to it, before the house by the bridge was built; and so to
> look about...

What better guide to walking London could there be?

Today, however, along with comfortable shoes and an ear cocked for an approaching double-decker bus, those seeking to explore

Pepys's London also need an active imagination. London has suffered two extinction-level events in her recent history. The first, the Great Fire of 1666, was witnessed by Pepys; the second, the Blitz of the Second World War, destroyed most of the sights and buildings in the old City that had somehow survived the first. Most, but not all: there are still rare survivors, which feature as stopping points on the five walks that form the body of this book; others can be imaginatively recreated, if the walkers of today are willing to pause and to abstract themselves from the tumult of the twenty-first century and perhaps (ever mindful of that pestilential traffic) to half-close an eye. London's historical blueprint is remarkably persistent, as if the older the stamp put upon her hills and fields and the banks of her river, the more stubbornly it remains. After the Fire of 1666, Londoners simply rebuilt on the same plots and to the same shapes the properties they had lost; and despite even the Blitz, there remains within the old City (which for our purposes we take as stretching roughly from Fleet Street to the Tower) the original pattern of many of her most significant streets and of her tiny linking alleyways and 'courts', such as the one where Pepys was born.

The same is true of Whitehall and Westminster, to a lesser extent, and along the banks of the Thames itself, while in Greenwich and Deptford, where Pepys – Clerk of the Acts to the Navy Board from July 1660 – strolled and bustled and occasionally plotted, there are still buildings and vistas that can bring seventeenth-century London vividly to life.

Even when the buildings and street plans are lost, the ghosts remain. When I bought my twenty-first-century flat on the Isle of Dogs (the peculiar teardrop of land that hangs down into the Thames like a uvula), I had to take out 'chancel insurance', as somewhere under the basement car park of my building lies the footprint of a church. An oil painting now in the Museum of London Dock-lands and dating from about 1620 shows the Isle of Dogs as Pepys must have seen it many a time from Greenwich: the flat fields, the shimmer of marsh, the sails of a windmill. And sure enough, top right, as the Thames makes its final swing eastward, there is a jumble of small buildings, like flotsam deposited at the river's bend, and among them, a church steeple.

*

To us, the London of Pepys's time would seem miniscule. From east to west, within its medieval and in some places Roman walls (still standing, here and there, in Pepys's day), the City proper measured a little under five kilometres or three miles across. Walk from Fleet Street down the Strand and enough of a gap would open before you for Westminster and Whitehall to count as a separate place. Covent Garden was a garden; Lincoln's Inn Fields was fields, Smithfields the same. The so-called Faithorne and Newcourt map of 1658 – perfectly if unknowingly timed to record London just before the Fire – shows one single street of houses north of Holborn and open countryside beyond. (Pepys knew William Faithorne, the map's engraver; one wonders if he owned a copy.) Ribbon development runs along Fenchurch Street out to a dinky little windmill. St James's Palace, today between Piccadilly and Pall Mall, sits in open space, with deer tossing their antlers before it. Looking behind you from St James's, the jumble of roofs of the City would still have been low-rise enough to echo in their lines the rise and fall of the land beneath. Those on Ludgate Hill stood higher, for example; St Paul's higher than everything else. Maybe half a million people would have answered 'London' if in 1660 you had asked them where was home.

Greater London today is forty-five miles or over seventy kilometres across, from Havering in the east to Hillingdon in the west, and its population sits at just over eight million and counting.

And, to us, a good deal of it would not have looked urban at all. There were still farms and old manor houses with their fields and gardens to be found east and west; there was open heath; above all there was the Thames, which still had its natural banks, so streets that ended at the water ended in the gentle slope of any ancient riverbank. In Pepys's time there were no stone embankments driving the grey-green waters along. At its height, the mighty tidal rise, untrammelled, reached the lawns of the townhouses of the great and stairs such as Dorset Stairs, or sloshed beneath the watermen's seats, where the famously foul-mouthed London watermen waited for business. It lapped, as it does today, at the hundreds of fragile timber jetties and reinforced quays that industrious Londoners had been boldly throwing out from the foreshore since the Bronze Age. At low tide, that inimitable Thames mud stretched for yards, with the occasional sandy beach to tempt the adventurous: the 'Strand' was named for one of them. And, in the seventeenth century, a dozen or more smaller rivers still flowed across the plain of London and through the old City into the Thames – including the Fleet, after which the street was named. Only two, the River Lea and Deptford Creek, are visible today. Londoners took water from them for drinking, washing, and industry, and used them as glorified wet bins into which everything unwanted could be and was discarded.

The river's only man-made obstacle was London Bridge, which was also the only bridge. We have lost almost entirely the character of such bridges in northern Europe today but, if you have ever battled your way across the ninety-five metres of the Ponte Vecchio in Florence, you will have some idea of London Bridge in Pepys's time, albeit writ small. London's bridge was 270 metres or nearly 900 feet long, with houses and shops on either side (some 200 of them) that might be seven storeys high, built ever wider, with gable after gable projecting one above another, like inverted houses of cards. These structures precariously overhung the river on one side and the central roadway on the other, creating a kind of timbered tunnel down the middle of the bridge. Traffic was marshalled in either direction with great strictness (and might ultimately be the origin of our quaint English habit of driving on the left), but even so, the crowds of shoppers and wanderers meant that it could take an hour to cross the bridge on foot – as long as it would take to walk east to west across the Stuart city in its entirety.

Anyone whose time was money, like Pepys, would have much preferred to cross the river by boat – indeed, preferred the river over the streets for travel *tout court*. 'And so by boat' occurs in the Diary with almost the same frequency as 'walked'. But the river held its own perils. When the tide was flowing out, the footings of London Bridge restricted the flow of water so much that there could be a two-metre drop under each arch, like going over a weir. 'Shooting the bridge' was, of course, wildly popular among London's daring youth, and Pepys himself speaks of being 'washed' as he went through the bridge early one morning in July 1665. The bridge was 'for wise men to pass over, and for fools to pass under', said a proverb of the day. In winter, that same obstruction to its flow meant the river upstream could sometimes freeze solid – this still being the period of the 'Little Ice Age', from the 1300s to the mid-1800s – or solid enough, at any rate, for Londoners to disport themselves more or less safely upon it. Below the bridge, the river would be thick with craft of every type, size, and use imaginable.

The top-heavy, overhanging nature of the buildings on London's bridge was repeated on dry land. Away from the public buildings – such as the halls of the livery companies, the few fashionable new developments such as Covent Garden and Lincoln's Inn Fields, or the great houses along the river (including Whitehall Palace, the oldest and biggest of them all) – the domestic architecture of Pepys's London, much of it Tudor, some far older, would strike us today as crazily fractal. Every storey of every house jutted out over the floor beneath, leaving only narrow ribbons of sky visible above your head and adding to the air of claustrophobic bustle down most streets. You can still see the same in York's famous Shambles and catch glimpses of it in London – for example, Crown Passage in St James's. The roads and any open spaces between buildings were sometimes cobbled, rarely paved, but were most often just grass or mud. There were no pavements; wheeled traffic was separated from pedestrians by posts, as in Paris or Florence today, but the walking space was also taken up by displays of goods set out in front of shops. One of the notable spills recounted in the Diary occurred on 15 December 1662, when the coach Pepys was travelling in knocked against a butcher's stall in Newgate Market. Two sides of beef ended up on the ground, with the butcher initially claiming forty shillings' or five pounds' worth of damage. Pepys (no fool) inspected the damage and got them to settle for a single shilling.

Around London's many markets, wheeled traffic would have come to a stop altogether when pigs or sheep or cattle or geese were being driven to market or the slaughterhouse, while two carts confronting each other on a narrow stretch of roadway could bring traffic on both sides to a standstill until the carters had settled the matter, usually with their fists. The narrowed streets were joined together by yet narrower alleyways, which might debouch into the neighbourly rumpus of a residential courtyard or the sudden calm of a graveyard and a church. Perhaps the one true method for the newcomer to find a way through the low-rise city would have been steeple to steeple. The map of 1658 shows ninety-nine churches in the City; the Great Fire of 1666 claimed eighty-seven of them. As for the London air, as a matter of course, it was pungent as a farmyard, near to the markets or no. The air pollution from the burning of sea coal was a national disgrace in which Londoners, in their perverse way, no doubt took a hearty pride – supposedly, when Londoners spat, they spat 'black'.

*

The family Pepys at Samuel's birth consisted of his father, John, a tailor, and mother, Margaret, daughter of a Whitechapel butcher. In all, there were eleven little Pepyses, Sam being the fifth, but by the time our hero was nine, only three other siblings were still alive: Thomas, Paulina, and the last baby, John. The Pepyses were middle class but only middling so, yet they had connections far grander than they, which were to be centrally important in the career of their eldest surviving son. The first of these was father John's aunt Paulina, who had married Sir Sidney Montagu and was the mother of Edward Montagu (later 1st Earl of Sandwich), an eight-year-old when Samuel Pepys was born. Then there were the Norfolk Pepyses, headed by another John, whose abilities as an administrator (did it run in the family?) had brought him into the service of Sir Edward Coke – one of the greatest English lawyers of the early seventeenth century – and, after Sir Edward's death, into that of his son, Sir Robert, who lived superbly out near Epsom. Another of his father's cousins, Richard Pepys, was high among the staff of Oliver Cromwell's Exchequer and might have helped Sam get one of his first jobs there, too, working for George Downing. They were a family of resourceful strivers, and they seem to have looked after their own.

It would be an error to think of Pepys's early life as being entirely London-girt. As an infant he had been sent to live with his nurse in Kingsland, now Dalston Kingsland but then more open fields. There were trips out to the Cokes's great house, Durdans, and to grammar school in Huntingdon, where another cousin worked as bailiff to the Montagus at their country seat of Hinchingbrooke. (Huntingdon Grammar School, founded in 1565 and now Hinchingbrooke School, also had Oliver Cromwell as a pupil.) Then, in Samuel's late teens, after he finished his schooling back in London at St Paul's School, there was Cambridge University. There never seems to have been any suggestion he follow his father's profession as a tailor, so you get the feeling his parents were educating this personable, diligent, and ambitious son to go up in the world. Then, in 1655, Samuel got married – not for social advantage, as might have been expected, but for love – to Elizabeth, the teenage daughter of a pair of French Protestants who had arrived in England essentially as refugees. Married life had begun, not entirely smoothly, in Pepys's bachelor apartment (possibly an attic above a gatehouse) in Whitehall, where he was clerking first for Edward Montagu, then also at the Exchequer for George Downing. But at the time the Diary begins, thanks to his Exchequer salary, the couple had moved to better lodgings in nearby Axe Yard (for more details, see Walk 1). And Pepys had also survived, in 1658, a major surgical procedure: being 'cut' to rid himself of a bladder stone (his 'old pain').

In between Pepys's schooling and the start of his career as a civil servant, England had declared and fought a civil war, executed a king, endured the years of the Protectorate, and been to war with the Dutch, the Irish, and the Scots. It had opened up settlements across the Atlantic – from Newfoundland to Maryland – and in the West Indies. And now, in January 1660, for those who could tell which way the tide was turning, it was about to welcome a new king back to its throne – and its capital city.

*

Pepys begins, in his first entry in his new diary on Sunday 1 January 1660:

> Blessed be God, at the end of the last year I was in very good health, without any sense of my old pain, but upon [unless] taking of cold. I lived in Axe Yard having my wife, and servant Jane, and no more in family than us three.

What Pepys doesn't say, of course, in any overt manner, is why he began keeping a diary at this point. As a clue to that, one has to look at the next paragraph: after confirming that his wife was not pregnant (poor Elizabeth started the new year with her period), he continues, 'The condition of the State was thus...' Cromwell was dead. His incompetent son, Richard – 'Tumbledown Dick' as he was known – was out of office and out of power. Parliament was in flux, and change was in the air – most significantly in the actions of that old warhorse General Monck, who happened (handily) to have the army in Scotland behind him. To a young man working in Whitehall with one foot upon the ladder, these were times worth recording; he himself was of enough potential interest to play, even if only in his own account of them, the hero. Others were doing the same: Pepys's friend John Evelyn kept a diary too, while the antiquarian John Aubrey recorded any number of swift pen portraits of the age and its doings, which would become his *Brief Lives*.

There's a pass-notes version of the Restoration of Charles II that has the king returning by universal accord and to unanimous acclaim after the dreary Puritan years of no dancing, no theatres, and no fun. The truth was much more complex. All the way through the Protectorate there had been plots both to restore Charles II and to assassinate him. There were double-dealings and double agents: Pepys had been a Cambridge student with one of the most notorious, the closet Royalist Samuel Morland, and knew Oliver Cromwell's canny spymaster, John Thurloe, too. When Pepys was still a child, his own father, John the tailor, had made a somewhat mysterious trip abroad, perhaps on private business for the Montagus, about which we know no more. Since Charles I's execution in 1649, Royalists had taken bloody revenge on their opponents in Holland; at home, the extremist Fifth Monarchists were waiting for the year 1666 to bring about the end of the world or the Kingdom of Heaven – or both. (When Pepys was a boy, he would frequently have heard a neighbour, the gloriously named radical 'Praise-God Barebone', preaching away in Fleet Street, until the local apprentices took exception.) With this the temper of the times, the fact that Pepys slipped into an idiosyncratic private 'code' (partly shorthand and partly a sort of Esperanto of his own) for sections of his Diary is perhaps not surprising. Cromwellian London was a censored society (as was London under Charles II), so Pepys was already in the habit, when Edward Montagu was out of London, of keeping the latter up to speed in private newsletters of his own composition. The segue from creating a newsletter to keeping a diary is easy. And Pepys was, above all, an administrator, and administrators turn the randomness of human activity into paper and ink to impose upon it sense and order. Pepys's Diary let him observe his own life, and thereby do the same.

Pepys had the character of a diarist. Leonardo da Vinci has been described as 'thinking' through his drawings; with Pepys it is perhaps that he came to understand a thing more fully if he had set it down in words – whether it was a piece of political sleight of hand or his own sex drive. He was diligent; he had application; he had a quotidian regularity of habit (*the* essential for a diarist). He had, perhaps, a slightly obsessive streak. Pepys couldn't see a system without seeking to improve it, and if he saw a thing done badly could not let it alone until it had come good. He was as perpetually improving the City house he was soon to move to, in Seething Lane, as he was refining the systems by which the Stuart navy built and outfitted its ships and equipped and paid its sailors.

He had the artistic sensibility of a writer too. We know that as a student he had written a fascinating-sounding composition entitled *Love A Cheat*, and he employs in his Diary the writer's trick of circling the world he has created to view it from whatever standpoint he desires: describing the meadows near Hinchingbrooke, he was to speak of them as 'the largest and most flowery spot the sun ever beheld'. Maybe it is less surprising that he began his Diary in the changing times of January 1660 than that he hadn't begun one before.

Pepys kept his Diary for nine years, until May 1669, when his fears for his eyesight caused him to lay it aside. He records in it both the Great Plague and the Great Fire, another war with the Dutch, the doings of his household, and the inner life of his own mind. It ended before he could record Elizabeth's death, in November 1669; it also does not cover his time as MP for Harwich, his two short periods of political imprisonment, or his travels to Tangier.

The years of his greatest professional triumphs were also still to come when he signed off the Diary for the last time, as was what might have been the most stable period in his emotional life, after Elizabeth's death, when he set up a household with Mary Skinner, the daughter of a neighbour in Mark Lane. Mary became well enough known and accepted in Pepys's circle to be referred to as 'Mrs Pepys' (his patron, Lord Brouncker, had much the same long-term set-up with his mistress, Abigail Williams).

Was Sam faithful to Mary, as he most certainly had not been to Elizabeth? As we walk, we will encounter the Martin sisters in Westminster, first of all; then there was Mrs Bagwell, down in Deptford, whose husband practically pimped her out to Pepys; there was the actress Elizabeth Knepp; there were any number of young shopwomen and barmaids who caught his eye and who were then pursued as a hunter pursues game – or, as we might say today, stalked. And there was his involvement with Deb Willet, which almost broke his marriage. He is candid about all of them, but in this area of his life, did he really not see what he was doing?

Because above all, Pepys is the watcher of himself, just as he watches the people in his household, or the grandees of Whitehall, or those he encounters on London's streets. Even in the throes of rage, he is taking note of his actions, as in the tumultuous argument with Elizabeth on 9 January 1663, in which both his will and her private papers end up scattered in torn-up pieces across the floor of their bedroom. He can step aside from himself: 'A great joy it is to me to see myself in good disposition', he writes approvingly on 1 March 1666, creating what one might call the 'first person once removed' to see it. This objectivity makes him more open and honest in his Diary than he might have let himself be in many of his conversations. What makes Pepys so valuable a commentator is that he had enough self-knowledge to examine himself, but not so much as to censor his feelings. What further sets him apart as a chronicler is that in linking writers and places one must so often allow for artistic licence – this fictional setting might equate with that real one, this be inspired by that event – but there is none of this with Pepys. These are the real locations of his life; this is exactly what he saw happening to himself in them, and through the Diary we revisit these places with him as our guide. He is, in a way, like that other great celebrant of all things London, the artist William Hogarth. Just as in Hogarth's paintings, with Pepys, everything is happening, all at once and everywhere.

Let's start walking.

Author's Note

ALL THE WALKS in this book, with the exception of Walk 4, should take about half a day to complete. For Walk 4, 'Along the River to Greenwich', I would set aside a whole day – and try to pick a day with good weather.

The details of left and right or north and south will, I hope, be adequate to find your way about, but I have anticipated that anyone following these walks will be doing so with a mobile phone in their pocket, and you may find yourself very grateful that you have it. Some of the alleyways in particular can be elusive the first time you set out to find them. The technologically savvy can also scan the QR code at the back of the book to access digital versions of the walking routes.

This book was written over the spring and summer of 2020, which presented very unusual challenges to anyone composing a selection of London walks, as well as helping me understand Pepys's emotions as he walked around the sad, silent, plague-ridden city of 1665. After the first lockdown, the face of the City had changed. Businesses used here as landmarks and as aids for orientation were promising to re-open, and I fervently hope that all of them have done so; churches, museums, and galleries likewise, changed or restricted opening times notwithstanding. It would only be sensible to check before you set out that any particular place you have in mind to visit will still be there and waiting for you.

From Westminster to the City

Somewhat perversely, you may feel, this walk will take you through Samuel Pepys's early life in reverse. Trust me, it makes a much better route that way. The walk starts in Westminster, where you have to imagine Samuel as he was when he began his Diary in January 1660 – already married to his Elizabeth but still only twenty-seven years old – and leads you back into the City and to Salisbury Court off Fleet Street, where he was born. It also takes you back from Stuart London, as it was coming into being thanks to visionaries such as the architect Inigo Jones, designer of Whitehall's Banqueting House, and into the far older Elizabethan city. On the way, this walk will take in some of the oldest, most beautiful, and most mysterious places in London: the Inns of Court.

Allow a good half-day for this walk, certainly if you spend time exploring the Inns of Court up Chancery Lane. Your reward at the end will be sinking into a seat in one of London's oldest taverns.

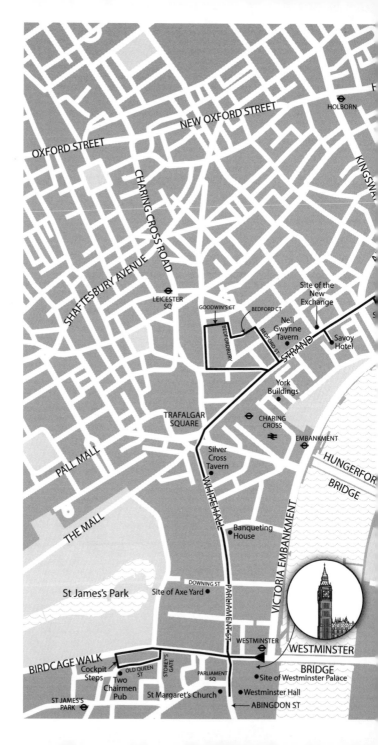

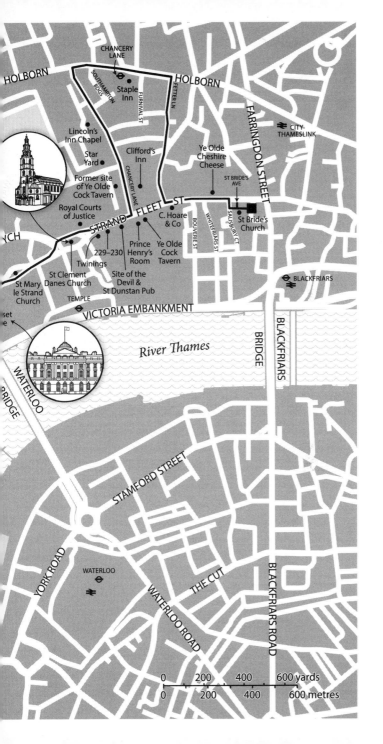

CHANCERY LANE

HOLBORN

HOLBORN

SOUTHAMPTON BLDGS

Staple Inn

FURNIVAL ST

FETTER LN

FARRINGDON STREET

CITY THAMESLINK

Lincoln's Inn Chapel

Star Yard

Clifford's Inn

Ye Olde Cheshire Cheese

ST BRIDE'S AVE

Former site of Ye Olde Cock Tavern

CHANCERY LANE

FLEET ST.

SALISBURY CT

St Bride's Church

Royal Courts of Justice

STRAND

C. Hoare & Co

BOUVERIE ST

WHITEFRIARS ST

YCH

229–230

Prince Henry's Room

Ye Olde Cock Tavern

BLACKFRIARS

Twinings

St Clement Danes Church

Site of the Devil & St Dunstan Pub

St Mary le Strand Church

TEMPLE

VICTORIA EMBANKMENT

BRIDGE

BLACKFRIARS

set e

River Thames

BLACKFRIARS

WATERLOO BRIDGE

STAMFORD STREET

WATERLOO

YORK ROAD

WATERLOO ROAD

THE CUT

BLACKFRIARS ROAD

| 0 | 200 | 400 | 600 yards |
| 0 | 200 | 400 | 600 metres |

Begin at Westminster Tube station, where you will find yourself surrounded by London at its most bustling: all the traffic streaming over Westminster Bridge, all the tourists milling around Big Ben and the Houses of Parliament. Go south, down Abingdon Street, and there on your left is Oliver Cromwell, standing proudly outside the very building whose power he did so much to create. Unsurprisingly, you would not have found his statue here in Pepys's day; instead you would have found his head, stuck on a pole six metres up in the air outside Westminster Hall. Hamo Thornycroft's statue of 1899 preserves only a suggestion of the famous wart on Cromwell's forehead, but it does show his great square jaw – a feature still clear in an eighteenth-century sketch of the famous skull itself. By January 1660, the smart thing to do was shake one's own head over the whole business of the Protectorship as a sad and baffling interlude in England's royal history. The first few months of 1660 were exciting times to be a young clerk watching events in Whitehall. Samuel writes on 2 March:

> Great also is the dispute now in the House, in whose name the writs shall run for the next Parliament; and it is said that Mr. Prin [William Prynne], in open House, said, 'In King Charles's.'

What's notable here is that the man Pepys describes as uttering such pro-royal sentiments had begun his political life as an outspoken Puritan, so outspoken in fact – fulminating against the drinking of toasts, at women cutting their hair, at men not cutting theirs – that in 1634 he was pilloried, fined, and had both his ears cut off. During the Civil War, he had supported the Parliamentarians; now here he was, stomping into Westminster Hall, armed unhandily with an old basket-hilted broadsword. It must have been a sight (especially when the sword tripped up another MP, Sir William Waller), and it would have confirmed beyond doubt that the days of the Protectorate were done. By the summer of that year, Charles II had been restored to his father's throne, and of the men who had put Charles I to death, those still living were facing the kind of executions not out of place on screen in *A Game of Thrones*, and those already dead had been pulled from their graves and had their heads displayed like Cromwell's outside Westminster Hall for all to gawp at. And it is that hall, behind Cromwell's statue, where we go next.

Westminster Hall is by far the oldest surviving part of the Houses of Parliament. When you look up at its astonishing hammer-beam roof, begun in 1393 for Richard II, you are looking at the largest medieval timber roof in Northern Europe – and seeing exactly what Pepys would have seen on any of his many visits to the hall. It's a breath-taking space, 73 metres (240 feet) long, the essence of history captured in timber and stone; to the visitor today, it seems to almost vibrate with all that has taken place here, including the trials of Sir Thomas More and Charles I himself. But in Pepys's day, the hall's floor space was also thronged with shoppers, stalls, and stall-holders, including Betty Martin. Pepys bought many a shirt from Betty, and he bought her many a bottle of wine in one or another of Whitehall's many taverns. Matters proceeded with Betty as one might expect; by 29 June 1663...

after great talk that she never went abroad with any man as she used heretofore to do, I with one word got her to go with me and to meet me at the further Rhenish wine-house, where I did give her a Lobster and do so touse [to ruffle or disorder] her and feel her all over, making her believe how fair and good a skin she has, and indeed she has a very white thigh and leg, but monstrous fat.

The Rhenish Wine House was on the right-hand side of Canon Row, which you will have passed on Bridge Street. Pepys also, in his phrase, 'did what he would' from time to time with Betty's sister, Doll.

While Westminster Hall has survived in all its grandeur, its surroundings have changed almost beyond recognition since Pepys knew them. New Palace Yard – which was home to the Turk's Head coffee-house, and Pepys's barber (and wigmaker) Richard Jervas – is now the green space north of Westminster Hall; Old Palace Yard is the car park below it. Parliament Street and Whitehall have replaced the main thoroughfare, as Pepys knew it, of King Street. Above all, we have lost the old Palace of Whitehall itself, an extraordinary accretion of buildings bigger even than the Vatican, which ran from Northumberland Avenue down to about the line of what is Downing Street today, and east to the banks of the Thames itself. So four entire blocks of today's city, regularly burned down, regularly rebuilt, constantly enlarged, until a final conflagration in 1698 swept it all away.

Of the old complex of Whitehall and Westminster as Pepys knew it, we do of course have Westminster Abbey and, just before the abbey, St Margaret's Church. There are several places encountered in these walks where really the reader could happily spend the rest of the day wandering up and down – Westminster Abbey is one of them, and it more than deserves all the books devoted to its history, so make a note to explore it with one of them to hand on another occasion. Pepys was to be found at the abbey on many a Sunday morning when he lived at Axe Yard but, for a personal Pepysian connection, St Margaret's is the place to go. It is here that Sam and Elizabeth were married, and this was the church frequented by many of their Axe Yard neighbours too. Here, on 5 August 1660, Pepys

heard the Book of Common Prayer, which had been banned under
the Protectorate, used again in church for the first time since 1649.
Whenever his business took him back to Westminster, even after
St Olave's in Hart Street had become 'our church', Sundays would
find him visiting his old haunt and his old habits. On Sunday 26
May 1667, he was nosing about Westminster Hall in search of Betty
Martin and, not finding her there, guessed that he might catch up
with her on her way to St Margaret's. A matter of seconds, and an
assignation was set up, but then –

> I met with Mr. Howlett [a Westminster shopkeeper and father
> to another Betty, Betty Mitchell, who had also caught Pepys's
> eye], who, offering me a pew in the gallery, I had no excuse
> but up with him I must go, and then much against my will
> staid out the whole church in pain while she [Betty Martin]
> expected me at home, but I did entertain myself with my
> perspective glass up and down the church, by which I had the
> great pleasure of seeing and gazing at a great many very fine
> women; and what with that, and sleeping, I passed away the
> time till sermon was done –

and the assignation could be kept.

St Margaret's is known as the parish church of the House of
Commons. It dates back to the mid-twelfth century and is 'a fair
parish church', as the historian John Stow describes it in his 1598
Survey of London, 'though sometime in danger of down-pulling'.
Indeed it was. In 1549 Edward Seymour, 1st Duke of Somerset, uncle
to the boy-king Edward VI, attempted to use its stones in the building
of Somerset House, which we will come to later. The angry parishioners refused to allow it, beating his workmen away with clubs.

The east window here, which was created perhaps in Flanders to celebrate the wedding of Henry VIII and Katherine of Aragon, dates to between 1515 and 1526. Hidden away after Henry divorced Katherine, it went first to Waltham Abbey, Essex, then after the Dissolution of the Monasteries to the private chapel of New Hall, Essex, a grand estate owned successively by the Boleyns, the 1st Duke of Buckingham, Oliver Cromwell, and General Monck. The window finally came into the possession of a Mr Conyers, who sold it to St Margaret's in 1758 for 400 guineas. All one can say is that these old windows must be a darn sight sturdier than they appear. Other reasons to love St Margaret's are that Barbara Villiers, mistress to Charles II and fantasy bedmate of Pepys, was christened here in 1641, and in 1647 the churchwardens were fined by those miserable Puritans for celebrating Christmas Day. Pepys's patron, Edward Montagu, married his Lady Jemima here, as did the poet John Milton his second wife in 1656; and William Caxton, Sir Walter Raleigh, and Wenceslaus Hollar (to whose engravings of seventeenth-century London any book on the period owes so much) are all buried here. As with so many London churches, it also has a plague pit.

Reverse your steps and go past the statue of Sir Winston Churchill, which conveniently marks the site of the Bell Tavern (and a 'special good dinner' in March 1660: 'a leg of veal and bacon, two capons and sausages and fritters, with abundance of wine') and walk along Birdcage Walk, with St James's Park on your right. Until 1828, only the royal family and their Hereditary Grand Falconer (the Duke of St Albans; the first duke was Charles II's son by Nell Gwyn) were permitted to drive along this wonderfully quiet road, deep in the green of the park's trees and still true to the original line set for it by Charles II. Perhaps because of that quietness, in the mid-nineteenth century it became something of a gay trysting ground. Note on your left Storey's Gate. Edward Storey was the keeper of Charles II's royal aviary in St James's Park, and his house was indeed next to the gate leading into the park – although not quite here. Keep a sharp eye out and next on your left are Cockpit Steps. The Royal Cockpit originally stood to the left of the steps. It too was built for Charles II, who revived cockfighting after it had been banned during the Commonwealth era – so not every idea those Puritans had was a bad one. It was eventually pulled down in 1810. Go up the steps to Old Queen Street, and as you do so you will see on your right a sort of half-pillar still bearing graffiti from that date and even earlier.

Old Queen Street was laid out in 1697. The plaque on Number 9 commemorates Richard Savage (1660–1712), the 4th Earl Rivers, who grew up to be a governor of the Tower of London and something of a military hero – though he had been such a Restoration rakehell as a youth that his own father, the 3rd Earl, once had him arrested for theft. The Two Chairmen pub, on the corner, commemorates the type of chairmen who carried sedan chairs – see the pub's sign – and in the 1680s, this corner was where one came to find a sedan chair much as today you might wait at a taxi rank. The domestic architecture here is that of late seventeenth-century London: confident, restrained, and uniform, very different to the scallywag higgledy-piggledy style of the Tudor buildings in the older City, with their repurposing of chunks of medieval masonry and even of Roman Londinium. You'll see houses very similar in Greenwich on Walk 4.

Now you'll need to work your way however you please back to Winston Churchill, turn left and go up Parliament Street. On the left is King Charles Street, where the site of Axe Yard and Pepys's house is now somewhere under the Foreign, Commonwealth & Development Office, and beyond that, Downing Street itself.

I can't get excited about Downing Street, for all its significance. Let us note only that it is named after Sir George Downing (1624/25–1684), 'master of my office', as Pepys described him in January 1660. Downing was, in fact, a proto-Yankee – his family lived in Massachusetts from 1638, he graduated from Harvard in 1642, and he helped negotiate the transfer of New York from the Dutch to the English on behalf of Charles II. He was also a penny-pinching turncoat and a hunter-down of his one-time Puritan colleagues in the first years of the Restoration. Let us shake him off and move on, heading toward Trafalgar Square.

Speaking of architectural changes, on your right you are coming up to Inigo Jones's Banqueting House. Much of 'new' Restoration London would have looked oddly Italian to us – like this perfect gem of a building, completed in 1622. In many ways it symbolises everything the first Stuarts wanted their rule to be: modern, harmonious, European, and unquestioned. Inside, no less an artist than Peter Paul Rubens created its ceiling paintings, which show the glories of the reign of James I, the first Stuart king, and in which James – looking to my mind like the astonished winner of some Baroque game show – is wafted up to heaven on an eagle. The reality was rather different. On 30 January 1649, his son King Charles I was walked from St James's Palace, where he was being held, across St James's Park, kept waiting for three hours inside his old apartment in Whitehall Palace, and then walked through the Banqueting House, under Rubens' genuflecting gods and goddesses, and out to his execution on a scaffold set up outside – witnessed as a schoolboy, of course, by one Samuel Pepys. (Do you see the bust of King Charles set above the entrance where visitors today walk in? That marks the window from which Charles stepped out to his death.)

There's a lot of historic score-settling in the northern half of

Whitehall. Looking down from Trafalgar Square is Hubert Le Sueur's sculpture of Charles I on horseback, shown not only triumphant but a deal taller than he ever was in life; also on this spot, the regicide Major-General Harrison was hung, drawn, and quartered on 13 October 1660. Of course, Sam was a witness to this too. He had recorded in his Diary the groan he remembered going up from the crowd when Charles I's head was shown to them in 1649, but when Harrison's head and heart were displayed to the waiting throng, 'there was [sic] great shouts of joy'.

In all this, don't miss, on your right, the Silver Cross Tavern. Before it was licensed as a tavern in 1674, the Silver Cross was licensed as a brothel; its licence as the latter was supposedly never revoked, so it now makes the claim to be the oldest licensed brothel in the United Kingdom. Certainly, this end of Whitehall – whether looked down on by Charles I or no – was in Pepys's day pretty rough and ready, lined with taverns of dubious reputation, the haunts of thieves, pickpockets and, later, highwaymen. Being wise, we will turn east – walking literally in Sam's footsteps all the way, since this route from Westminster back into the City was pretty much his daily constitutional – and turn into the Strand, marvelling as we do that looking north from Charing Cross in 1659, surrounded by the churchyard of St Martin-in-the-Fields, you would have been looking right along the western edge of the City of London and out to fields and open countryside beyond. (You would also have been close-ish, standing here, to the premises of Elizabeth Pepys's tailor and dressmaker, John Unthank.)

Equally amazing is the fact that in the 1660s, as you walked up the Strand, visible between the buildings at the end of every street sloping down to the river, there would have been a broad expanse of bright sand. The riverbank was much closer to you then than it is now, post the creation of the Victoria Embankment. If you wish to prove this to yourself, turn down the tatty little opening to Buckingham Street (how George, Duke of Buckingham, whose grand London house was one of many here along the Strand, would be appalled!) and walk down to the Victoria Embankment Gardens. Look through the railings and there is the York Watergate in front of you, marking where the edge of the river lapped at the edge of the gardens of York House, the Buckinghams' London seat. Buckingham Street was built over the site of the house in about 1675, and towards the end of his public life Pepys lived at two addresses here: first at Number 12, York Buildings, from 1679 to 1688, and then at Number 14 from 1688 to 1701, as the two plaques to him attest. Pepys, moneyed, leisured, long a widower, involved himself with gusto in the doings of the Royal Society and its latest scientific discoveries while he was living here. A letter has survived, addressed to him from his close friend and fellow diarist John Evelyn:

For Samuel Pepys Esqr at his lodging in York-streete

8 June 1684

Sir ...

Mr Flamsteed [the Astronomer Royal] has lately advertized me of an eclipse of the moone which will happen on the 17th of this month about 3 in the morning, and wished I would give you notice of it, that if your leasure permitted he might have the honor of your company, and I should readily waite upon you.

Your most humble and faithfull servant John Evelyn

As well as gatherings of the Royal Society (he was its president from 1684 to 1686, which must have delighted him), Pepys also held musical evenings here. He adored music as much as he loved books. On 19 April 1687, you might have stood here, looking out over the river from the open windows of Number 12, and heard the voice of the sensationally famous castrato Siface, performing for, as Evelyn recorded it,

> a select number of some particular persons whom Mr Pepys
> (Secretary of the Admiralty & a great lover of Musick) invited
> to his house, where the meeting was, & this obtained by peculiar
> favour & much difficulty of the Singer, who much disdained to
> shew his talent to any but Princes.

In 1698, Tsar Peter the Great, who we will also encounter in Greenwich, was a neighbour here. But by 1701 Pepys, now in fragile health, had joined his one-time servant Will Hewer in the latter's house out in the then countryside on Clapham Common. Hewer was in many ways Pepys's professional successor, and his fortune grew to be even greater than Sam's. Pepys was cared for with great devotion and much comfort in Clapham, where he died in 1703.

York House was but one of many palatial London homes along the Strand. There was Durham House, Bedford House, Arundel House, and Somerset House too. They made the Strand a highly fashionable part of London, even more so after Inigo Jones began developing Covent Garden for the Bedford family, with its Italian-looking piazza, and the building of the so-called 'New Exchange', a double-height colonnaded run of luxury shops opened in 1609 but demolished a century later. Before we get to Somerset House, however, cross the Strand and go up Bedford Street, and left through Bedford Court to Bedfordbury. Between Numbers 23 and 24, insert yourself into the unsavoury-looking passageway of Goodwin's Court. This is a true seventeenth-century survivor, dating from 1690, complete with gas lighting and an original badge, shaped like a bishop's cap, above you on the wall as you enter, the insignia of one of the first private London fire brigades. One of London's many legends has Nell Gwyn living here in her orange-seller days; it is also by repute the inspiration for Diagon Alley in the Harry Potter books.

I would heartily recommend that whenever one of these little alleyways or courts strikes your eye as you perambulate around London in Sam's footsteps, you investigate it. You never know what you will find. For example, if on your way back to the Strand you turn off Bedford Street and onto Maiden Lane (where the poet Andrew Marvell was living in 1677 and where the painter J. M. W. Turner was born in 1775, above his dad's barber's shop at what is now Number 21), you can walk down Bull Inn Court, also supposedly a seventeenth-century survivor, which has the 'Nell Gwynne' pub at its far end. Or, carry on down Maiden Lane to Southampton Street: this is where the painter John Hayls was living when he painted Samuel Pepys. His portrait of Pepys, and those of many of the other individuals mentioned in the Diary, can be found in the National Portrait Gallery, and I recommend a visit there, too. As with London's alleyways and passages, the chance to spend time in her museums and galleries should never be neglected. For now, though, make your way back to the Strand however you please and on we go to the Savoy – not then a hotel, as it is now, but rather the remains of another grand palace, fallen into sad disrepair. Part of it was a sort of public hospital, cluttered with shops and 'vagabonds' who spent the day lying around in the hospital gardens. On the evening of 8 August

1661, Pepys was in a tavern next to the Savoy drinking with Henry Madge, one of the royal violinists, and witnessing an argument, as it turned out, about whether the French or English were the more musical nation. Pepys was also known at our next port of call, the last survivor of the palaces of the Strand: Somerset House itself. '[T]hence to Somerset House', he writes on 24 February 1664,

> and there into the chapell ... now it is made very fine and was
> ten times more crowded than the Queen's chapell at St James's,
> which I wonder at. Thence down to the garden of Somerset
> House, and up and down the new building, which in every
> respect will be mighty magnificent and costly.

Really nothing but the size of the site survives from its earlier incarnations, as all the buildings round you if you visit Somerset House today are from the eighteenth or nineteenth century. But if you step inside its courtyard and maybe half-close an eye, you can begin to get some idea of the style and magnificence with which life in these enormous riverside palaces would have been lived. Protector Somerset built the first palace here in 1547; it was home to James I's queen, Anne of Denmark, and later to Charles I's queen, Henrietta Maria; Inigo Jones died here; Cromwell lay in state. Both the Royal Society and the Navy Office, where Pepys once worked, were housed here after the eighteenth-century rebuilding. The best thing about it today is that it is home to the Courtauld Gallery, which is again well worth a visit in its own right, and whose Old Master paintings and superlative Impressionist collection make a spiritual connection at least to the astonishing array of paintings and other treasures that would have been held in London's original riverside palaces at their height.

Carry on along the Strand, past St Mary le Strand – a perfectly nice little church, but built in 1714, so of no importance to us here – and, as you pass the disused Strand Tube station, note the tiny plaque on the wall commemorating William Lilly. Lilly lived in a house here from 1627 to 1665, working on his *Christian Astrology*, a monster of a book which has never been out of print since its first publication in 1647. Sam was inclined to dismiss astrology ('a great many fooleries, which may be done by nativities', he writes in October 1660), although reading Lilly's prophecies of 'great expectations for Peace' at home and 'loss at sea' for Holland during the disastrous June of 1667 did at least give Sam and Will Hewer a laugh of sorts: the Dutch seemed to be carrying all before them, the English navy, unpaid, was on the point of mutiny, and London was in such confusion that Pepys could only compare it to the nights of the Great Fire.

Walk on to the second church, sitting on its little island amongst the traffic of the Strand, and, as you reach it, notice how all those crowds of people that were thronging every other part of this walk have simply disappeared. This church is St Clement Danes, and the small miracle of the disappearing tourists is one it performs on a daily basis. It is also one of the two St Clements that claim the right to utter the words 'oranges and lemons' in the traditional rhyme – the other is St Clement's Eastcheap. Pepys's cousin Jane Turner (in whose house he had endured that operation to remove his kidney stone in 1657) lodged close by here for a while, until her husband ordered her back north; and here, in June 1665, 'in the open street', Pepys saw one of the first houses to be shut up because of the plague. Supposedly, the name of the church refers back to a small community of Danes who had married English women in the time of Alfred the Great and so were allowed to live and worship here. Dr Johnson worshipped here too, many centuries later, and his presence should give you a clue that we are now entering a part of London where words have always counted for a great deal.

The interior of St Clement Danes is large and light and galleried, restrained whilst being opulent, but my favourite part of it is the Rubik's Cube of its steeple, which always seems to be asking to be twitched right to align it perfectly. The church survived the Great Fire, but by 1679 it was falling down, so Sir Christopher Wren rebuilt it; the steeple of 1719 was created by James Gibbs.

We are now coming up to a part of the walk where places of interest come particularly thick and fast. First is the half-timbered George pub, founded in 1723 as a coffee shop but cunningly looking far older. Dr Johnson used the George as a postal address for a while. And where there is coffee, there must be tea – almost next door is Twinings tea shop, which is London's oldest shop to remain in its original location, having been here since 1706, and good Lord, where would we writers be without our cups of tea? Pepys first drank tea on 25 September 1660 – 'a China drink', he calls it – and the figures of the two Chinese mandarins here remind us that until the mid-nineteenth century, all tea came from China. In between the two is another of those intriguing alleyways; this one leads to the Devereux pub. If you investigate, the dark red bust looking down from the pub's top storey is of Robert Devereux, 3rd Earl of Essex (1591–1646), who was the original commander of the Parliamentarian army in the English Civil War. Essex was the victim of two notoriously unhappy marriages, with public accusations of impotence and adultery entertaining court and commoner for decades; one wonders if he turned to soldiering as a relief.

Then, at 229–230 the Strand, with a wonderfully patchworked leaded light window and proudly jutting upper storey, you come to the first genuine domestic survivor from before the Great Fire. The building dates from 1625 and for many years was home to the Wig and Pen Club for lawyers and writers. The Thai restaurant that is the building's current occupier is alleged to share it with the headless ghost of Oliver Cromwell, perhaps an allusion to the fact that the building was originally erected to house the gatekeeper for Temple Bar Gate, and Temple Bar Gate was one of the many places where the heads of those executed were put on display. The site of the gate, which is now itself in Paternoster Square (see Walk 2), is marked a little further on by the huge and very handsome statue of a griffin (or is it a Tudor Dragon?) standing on high in the centre of the road, the griffin being the City's unofficial badge and Temple Bar Gate marking the City's official western edge, the point where the Strand becomes Fleet Street. 'Up', Pepys records on 15 May 1667...

> and with Sir W. Batten and [Sir] J. Minnes to St. James's, and
> stopt at Temple Bar for Sir J. Minnes to go into the Devil's
> Taverne to shit, he having drunk whey, and his belly wrought.

Sir William Batten was another naval administrator (and the MP for Rochester); Sir John Mennes the same, but also a wit and excellent companion; the 'Devil' we will come to below.

Continue past the Royal Courts of Justice, and on the left you'll see Bell Yard, the original site of Ye Olde Cock Tavern, now to be found a little way further down the street on the right. Pepys might often have been encountered here, eating lobster and making merry with the actress Mrs Knepp and Mrs Pearse (wife of the surgeon James Pearse and another favourite of his, at least until September 1667, when she began to 'paint' – 'so that henceforth to be sure I shall loathe her'). At least once, he brought poor Elizabeth here too (one can only hope the barman had been bribed to keep quiet). After a merry evening that began here on 23 April 1668, making his way home via St Dunstan in the East, close by Seething Lane, he narrowly avoided being mugged:

> walking towards home, just at my entrance into the ruines at St. Dunstan's, I was met by two rogues with clubs, who come towards us. So I went back, and walked home quite round by the wall, and got well home, and to bed weary, but pleased at my day's pleasure.

He might have suffered a far worse fate: Bell Yard's real claim to fame is that in the 1846 penny dreadful magazine story 'The String of Pearls' – the sensational yarn that gave the world Sweeney Todd, the Demon Barber of Fleet Street – Mrs Lovett's pie shop was here in Bell Yard, with the barber's shop itself next door by St Dunstan's Church.

St Dunstan-in-the-West, which we come to next, escaped the Great Fire and is as historic as a church can be: William Tyndale, who went on to translate the Bible into English, gave 'lectures' here; the great metaphysical poet John Donne, who coined the phrase 'no man is an island', was rector here (there is a bust of him inside the church); Izaak Walton was a 'sidesman', or churchwarden's assistant, here, and his delightful *Compleat Angler* was published in 1653 by a local printer, Robert Marriot, who sold books in the churchyard. Then, to lower the tone completely, along comes Sam in August 1667:

> ... [I] turned into St. Dunstan's Church, where I heard an able sermon of the minister of the place; and stood by a pretty, modest maid whom I did labour to take by the hand and the

body; but she would not, but got further from me; and, at last, I could perceive her to take pins out of the pocket to prick me if I should touch her again – which seeing I did forbear, and was glad I did spy her design. And then I fell to gaze upon another pretty maid in a pew close to me, and she on me; and I did go about to take her by the hand, which she suffered a little and then withdrew. So the sermon ended, and the church broke up, and my amours ended also...

St Dunstan's also has a magnificent clock outside – the first public clock in London to have a minute hand. The two giants traditionally associated with London, Gog and Magog, hammer out the hours and turn their heads as they do so. It dates from 1671, and it's thought to have been set up by the parishioners in gratitude for their church having been spared when so many were destroyed by the Great Fire. Inside, the present church is rather surprising: octagonal in shape, it has a Romanian Orthodox connection and thus a huge iconostasis on the left-hand wall.

St Dunstan's gave its name to another of Pepys's favourite Fleet Street taverns, with the memorable name of the Devil and St Dunstan. A medieval legend tells how St Dunstan, the patron saint of goldsmiths, spotted the Evil One lurking in his workshop and seized him at once by the nose with a pair of red-hot pincers. The Devil gave him no more trouble thereafter, and St Dunstan went on to become Archbishop of Canterbury. The pub, which seems to have been on the south side of Fleet Street, and more or less midway between 229–230 Strand and Chancery Lane, must have been immense: it's recorded for tax purposes as having nineteen hearths and was patronised by the playwright Ben Jonson. Pepys knew one of its owners, John Wadlow, by name. One wonders if Pepys had the legend of St Dunstan in mind in the wee small hours of 12 January 1669 when his wife, maddened with jealousy and misery at the thought of her husband's amours with Deb Willet, stood at the side of his bed brandishing fire tongs 'red hot at the ends'. Fortunately the episode ended with no harm done.

The entrance to Chancery Lane is where you need to situate yourself next. Once you are there, look opposite, and you will see the timbered front of the so-called Prince Henry's Room, again with that unmistakable jutting top storey and a huge stone gate beneath it, leading to the grounds of Temple Church and the Middle Temple (which we will visit on Walk 3). Pepys knew this building too, but as the Fountain Tavern. The main room above the gateway dates from 1610 and preserves its original panelling as well as a splendid decorative plaster ceiling. On tiptoe, you might glimpse some of the ceiling from the pavement and judge how breathtaking it is for yourself. Its name, though, may be a bit of canny marketing rather than recording any actual royal connection. And this is where we leave Fleet Street behind us and turn north, up Chancery Lane.

The entirety of this part of London, spanning north to Holborn and south to the river, is given over to the study and practice of law – and it has been thus for centuries. Indeed, this is why the printers and booksellers and later (before they all decamped to Wapping) the newspapers set up shop here: because this is where you found the literate professions, the lawyers and the clergy, who had need of them. Jacob Tonson, the bookseller who ended up with the copyright (once such a thing had been brought into legal existence) for both Shakespeare's Fourth Folio and Milton's *Paradise Lost*, and who would certainly have been known to Pepys, set up shop here at the Fleet Street end of Chancery Lane in 1678. He was one of many. The entrance to Clifford's Inn, encountered on your right as you head up Chancery Lane, was also certainly here in their time, Clifford's Inn having been the first of the Inns of Chancery, set up in 1344. Wander into the pretty little garden and round to the right and you can still see its early nineteenth-century gatehouse, even if the inn was demolished in the 1930s. On the Fleet Street side of the gatehouse, there is a stone plaque dated 1682 – preserved with no clue as to how or why, but a tap on the shoulder from Pepysian London nonetheless.

The appearance of the word 'inn' in the names of so many of these lawyerly sites in London seems to stem quite simply from the fact that those who lived, worked, and studied here were given bed and board in these institutions, just as if they had in fact been inns. But what they always remind visitors of most strongly are so many Cambridge or Oxford colleges – as though they've been dropped down into the hubbub of London. They give this part of London a particular quality of calm and stillness, as if the rest of the city around them has ceased to exist. And oh my word, they are old. Lincoln's Inn, which will be coming up on your left (and which is not to be confused with Lincoln's Inn Fields, next door to it), was founded significantly before 1420. If it looks familiar, this may be because it was the serene setting where *The Children Act* was filmed in 2016. Its Old Square was built between 1525 and 1609, its Old Hall begun in 1489, and the present chapel was built by Inigo Jones between 1620 and 1623. In 1659, its undercroft hosted a secret meeting of eighty members of parliament to discuss the restoration of the monarchy. Pepys was in Lincoln's Inn very frequently on this or that knotty legal problem, usually for Downing, but it's Lincoln's Inn Fields that is found much more frequently in the Diary because there was a theatre there – so we will save that for Walk 3. There are tours of the buildings of Lincoln's Inn, and the lawns and gardens are open to visitors, but the staff are rightly very security conscious, so be on your best behaviour. Keep the peace, in every way.

There is a passageway off New Square Garden in Lincoln's Inn that (if it is open) will take you down to Carey Street, which is also well worth exploring. The Silver Mousetrap jewellers at Number 56 boasts of having been established in 1690; the Seven Stars pub beside it has been there since 1602. The statue of Sir Thomas More celebrates him as a member of Lincoln's Inn Fields and dates from 1866. And if you then walk along Carey Street back to Chancery Lane, you will come to the Knights Templar pub on the corner. The Temple Church, built south of Fleet Street in 1162 by the Knights Templar (and also saved for Walk 3), is what gives the whole area of 'the Temple' its name.

We will now turn back up Chancery Lane, pushing on northward still, past the London Silver Vaults (more retail therapy for the seriously silver-minded). Turn right onto High Holborn and continue on almost to Chancery Lane Tube station. On your right is the gate to Staple Inn, through which you may glimpse the courtyard described in Dickens's *The Mystery of Edwin Drood* as

> one of those nooks, the turning of which out of the clashing
> street imparts to the relieved pedestrian the sensation of having
> put cotton in his ears, and velvet soles on his boots.

The description could be applied to any of the Inns in this part of London. But what I want you to do next is look up and gasp, for there, rising up over Chancery Lane, is Staple Inn itself – not one Tudor building but an entire run of them, zebra-striped in black and white; when we come to explore Cheapside or any of the other great historic streets of the City in Walk 2, this is what you should hold in your head and multiply up and down, on either side. Originally constructed in the 1580s, their surprisingly unrickety appearance is owing, I suspect, to the steel frame that was cunningly inserted into their Tudor fabric in the 1930s to strengthen them. These buildings are a drop of precious architectural DNA, if you like, from which your imagination can clone seventeenth-century London.

Now continue east along Holborn, past Furnival Street and the narrow alleyway of Dyer's Buildings, and turn right down the equally narrow opening to Fetter Lane (off which is Dr Johnson's House, where he created his dictionary) to get back to Fleet Street. Journey's end is in sight. As you re-enter Fleet Street, you will see in front of you C. Hoare & Co., the UK's oldest privately owned bank, founded in 1672. Hoare's was Pepys's bank from the 1680s onward, and Will Hewer's too, but in the 1660s what is now C. Hoare & Co. was the site of the Mitre Tavern. Pepys was boozing here with Captain Philip Holland on 18 February 1660:

> he took me to the Mitre in Fleet Street, where we heard (in a room over the music room) very plainly through the ceiling. Here we parted and I to Mr. Wotton's, and with him to an alehouse and drank while he told me a great many stories of comedies that he had formerly seen acted, and the names of the principal actors, and gave me a very good account of it.

Philip Holland was later to go over to the Dutch – the traitor! – but he then became a double agent spying for the English. The stage-struck 'Mr Wotton' was Pepys's shoemaker, William Wotton, and one imagines he went home after this evening in the alehouse to nearby Shoe Lane.

Now carry on down Fleet Street, past Bouverie Street and the

Tipperary pub (which looks as narrow as if it had been corseted), past Whitefriars Street, and next on your right is Salisbury Court itself and the plaque announcing Samuel's birthplace to the world. John Pepys, Sam's father, did his tailoring here, and indeed you have to imagine this area as being full of houses and workshops of all sorts, with yards and gardens running down to the river. If you then go down St Bride's Avenue, there before you will be St Bride's Church. St Bride's is one of the oldest sites of Christian worship in London, and it is known as 'Fleet Street's church', with a centuries-long association with newspapers and journalists and the written or printed word. In 1500, the quite brilliantly named Wynkyn de Worde (of whom more in Walk 2) set up his printing press roughly opposite the church; its other claim to fame is that its wedding-cake steeple is said to have inspired the design of wedding cakes since 1703, when a lovelorn local baker created the first such tiered cake. The steeple (dated between 1701 and 1703) would have been very new then; the rest of the church beneath, which is another of Wren's, dates from 1675. Pepys was baptised here in the previous, pre-Great Fire church on 3 March 1633 and, in his honour, I think it's time to wet the baby's head.

You have a choice of three taverns in which to do so: Ye Olde Cock Tavern, which has moved from the site where Pepys knew it but still has the fireplace and overmantel preserved from the original building; the Tipperary, which is a great Fleet Street boozer in its own right; or Ye Olde Cheshire Cheese, which might, in parts at least, date back to 1538, when there was an inn here too. Sir Arthur Conan Doyle drank here, as did Dickens, who mentions it in *A Tale of Two Cities*, and Dr Johnson. While it isn't in the Diary, I would be confounded to find Pepys wasn't here as well. The pub's stuffed pet parrot, Poll, who is still in her favourite place above the bar, died in 1939, but she is remembered for her habit of flying about the saloon bar squawking 'f*** the Kaiser!' Whichever watering hole you choose, you have covered a good seven kilometres or some four-and-a-half miles to get here. Cheers!

WALK 2

Through the City to Seething Lane

THIS WALK PICKS UP roughly where Walk 1 left off. It will take you from Blackfriars into the heart of the old City, from St Paul's Cathedral up to Smithfield and one of London's oldest and loveliest churches, down again to the Guildhall, to Bank and what was the old City's shopping centre, and finally to the streets around Samuel and Elizabeth's home in Seething Lane. As it is, it covers about seven kilometres (four-and-a-half miles) and is another walk for a half-day but, if you wish, by cutting ahead to Walk 5, you can extend it along the river on its north bank to Wapping and end at any one of three historic pubs.

Before we begin, a word of advice. As we discovered in Walk 1, the old City of London is tiny. Even in Pepys's day, it still sat pretty comfortably within its Roman walls: from Ludgate in the west, where we begin, up to Newgate and Aldersgate, round to Cripplegate, Moorgate, Bishopsgate, and so on to Aldgate in the east. The shortness of the distances on the ground deceives one's inner Fitbit: from experience, if you can't locate a particular landmark or building, it will inevitably be waiting right behind you.

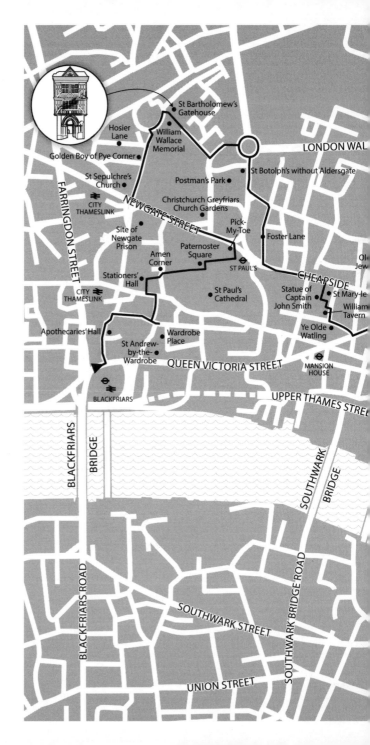

St Bartholomew's
Gatehouse

Hosier
Lane

William
Wallace
Memorial

Golden Boy of Pye Corner

LONDON WAL

St Sepulchre's
Church

Postman's Park

St Botolph's without Aldersgate

CITY
THAMESLINK

NEWGATE STREET

Christchurch Greyfriars
Church Gardens

FARRINGDON STREET

Site of
Newgate
Prison

Pick-
My-Toe

Foster Lane

Amen
Corner

Paternoster
Square

Ole
Jew

Stationers'
Hall

ST PAUL'S

CHEAPSIDE

CITY THAMESLINK

St Paul's
Cathedral

Statue of
Captain
John Smith

St Mary-le

William
Tavern

Apothecaries' Hall

Wardrobe
Place

Ye Olde
Watling

St Andrew-
by-the-
Wardrobe

QUEEN VICTORIA STREET

MANSION
HOUSE

BLACKFRIARS

UPPER THAMES STREE

BLACKFRIARS

BRIDGE

SOUTHWARK

BRIDGE

BLACKFRIARS ROAD

SOUTHWARK STREET

SOUTHWARK BRIDGE ROAD

UNION STREET

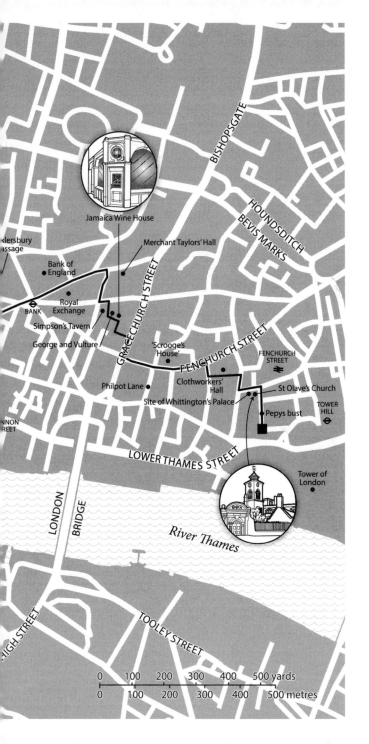

Jamaica Wine House

Merchant Taylors' Hall

klersbury assage

Bank of England

BISHOPSGATE

HOUNDSDITCH

BEVIS MARKS

Royal Exchange

BANK

Simpson's Tavern

George and Vulture

GRACECHURCH STREET

'Scrooge's House'

FENCHURCH STREET

FENCHURCH STREET

Philpot Lane

Clothworkers' Hall

St Olave's Church

Site of Whittington's Palace

Pepys bust

TOWER HILL

NNON REET

LOWER THAMES STREET

Tower of London

LONDON BRIDGE

River Thames

HIGH STREET

TOOLEY STREET

0   100   200   300   400   500 yards
0   100   200   300   400   500 metres

Start by coming out of Blackfriars tube station onto Queen Victoria Street. Directly in front of you will be the Blackfriar public house, looking like a miniature version of the Flatiron in New York, and right beside that is Black Friars Lane. This entire area takes its name from the black cloaks worn by the Dominican friars who had a priory here before Henry VIII stepped in. Walk up Black Friars Lane and, on your right, with a particularly handsome doorway, you will see the Apothecaries' Hall. What was an apothecary? Think of today's chemists and pharmacists. Pepys had recourse to one, a John Battersby (who became Master of the Society of Apothecaries in 1674), on 9 February 1663, when he had to take a day off work having given himself a 'disorder of the blood' by over-indulging in Polish gherkins:

> Could not rise and go to the Duke, as I should have done with
> the rest, but keep my bed and by the Apothecary's advice, Mr.
> Battersby, I am to sweat soundly...

The Society of Apothecaries is one of London's livery companies. These companies grew out of the medieval guilds and existed to regulate trade and tradesmen within the City. They were (most of them) very wealthy institutions, and they built halls to match. Most of the original sixteenth- and seventeenth-century halls fell victim to either the Great Fire, later redevelopment, or the Luftwaffe – or the fact that the trades they existed to protect simply no longer exist. Thirty-nine halls, however, are still in use today. The Apothecaries' Hall, which was itself rebuilt after 1666 and refaced in the eighteenth century, is the oldest survivor of them all.

Turn right from Black Friars Lane to Carter Lane, which is very pleasing in its own right (and even has a gutter running down the centre of the street, exactly as it would have done in the seventeenth century), and pause where Carter Lane is joined by St Andrew's Hill. You are now in what was the area of the Royal Wardrobe. As a tailor, Pepys's father would have been very familiar with this quarter; indeed, he tried once to get a job in the Royal Wardrobe, where the great robes of state and most significant items of royal couture were kept. The church of St Andrew-by-the-Wardrobe, down the hill if you wish to pay it a visit, celebrates with its name what the area used to be most famous for, and in the church is a memorial to William Shakespeare, who had a house in this parish while he worked at the Blackfriars Theatre. If you spotted a 'Playhouse Yard' on your way up Black Friars Lane, Blackfriars is the playhouse it remembers and, according to Peter Cunningham's invaluable 1840 *Handbook of London*, the yard marks the theatre's rough site.

For now, however, double back slightly and walk up Creed Lane, on your immediate right, to Ludgate Hill (and note in the word 'creed' the continuing emphasis on the written or printed word in this part of London, as in Walk 1). Another left, then a quick right, takes you up Stationers' Hall Court to Stationers' Hall. This is another of the City livery companies, and again the original hall burned down in the Great Fire, was rebuilt in the 1670s, and has been remodelled since. On its exterior wall, the hall has a plaque commemorating the same Wynkyn de Worde we met on Walk 1. Originally a German immigrant, de Worde joined the printer William Caxton in business, took over Caxton's presses on his death in *c.*1491, and went on to print everything from religious works to children's books, popularising the use of illustrations and introducing italic type, among many other innovations. And he also set up one of the first bookstalls – perhaps the very first – in St Paul's Churchyard.

Walk out onto Ave Maria Lane (this part of London does have some of the loveliest street names) and, if you wish, take another little detour left down Amen Corner, where you will see a run of surviving seventeenth-century houses, built for the clergy of St Paul's. Otherwise, find your way to Paternoster Square on the other side of Ave Maria Lane. In Pepys's day, when it was Paternoster Row, this had become – thanks to Wynkyn – pretty much the centre of bookselling in the capital (an offshoot was Duck Lane, now the top half of Little Britain). Joshua Kirton, from whom Pepys bought most of his books ('my bookseller', Pepys called him) was based here. On 26 September 1666, after the Fire, Pepys was deeply saddened to hear of

> the great loss of books in St. Paul's Church-yarde, and at their
> [Stationers'] Hall also, which they value about 150,000*l*.
> [pounds Sterling]; some booksellers being wholly undone,
> among others, they say, my poor Kirton.

As well as the stalls of the booksellers, Paternoster Row was surrounded by shops, many of which seem to have been haberdashers', selling cloth and trimmings (their hall is in Smithfield, where we will find ourselves shortly, though it is now a completely modern building). Pepys bought green moiré silk here for a 'vest' for himself, some striped silk for a petticoat for Elizabeth, and later some exotic camelhair cloth for a man's coat. Today the square is mostly devoted to cafes, but it does include a very pleasing sculpture by Elisabeth Frink (*Paternoster*) and Temple Bar Gate. This is the gate, referred to in Walk 1, that originally marked where the Strand became Fleet Street and which was one of the ceremonial entrances to the City. It was rebuilt many times in its history and, in the form in which we see it today, was probably designed by – you guessed it – Sir Christopher

Wren. But even that connection couldn't save it when it became too small and low for nineteenth-century traffic. Dismantled in 1878, it lived for many years in the grounds of Theobalds Park in Hertfordshire, only moving back here in 2004.

It may seem completely perverse, being so close here, not to go into St Paul's Cathedral, but St Paul's is another of those sites that deserves a day to itself, if not a lifetime, so give it its due on another occasion. (There is a sort of compensation coming up soon, in the form of the church of St Bartholomew the Great.) It's enough to say that there has been some kind of place of worship on this site since 604, and that the cathedral as we see it now is the fifth; Pepys saw the fourth burn during the Great Fire and be almost entirely rebuilt by Sir Christopher Wren during his lifetime, and with that I will leave you to get to know this exceptional monument in your own time. I would encourage you, however, to think what it must have been like for Londoners as they returned to their city after the Fire not to have the bulk of Old St Paul's rising above them; as traumatic for them, perhaps, as the altered skyline of Manhattan would have been for New Yorkers after 9/11. Now, make your way out of the square and along the present Paternoster Row to Panyer Alley. Turn left up the alley, past St Paul's Tube station, and onto Cheapside. As you come out of the alley you'll see on the wall on your left a much-eroded stone panel, showing a small boy astride what is indeed a pannier (or basket), who is known traditionally, for reasons that will become obvious on inspection, as 'Pick-My-Toe'. In fact, he is resting after carrying his basket of fresh-baked bread to the panel's original site on Ludgate Hill, as in the inscription from 1688. John Stow's *Survey* describes how the bakers of Stratford would bring their carts into the City daily to sell bread, and our small friend here is a pannier boy, a street seller employed by a baker to sell fresh bread to passers-by.

If you look left, you will see the ruins of another church, which have been converted into a delightful garden with tall open wooden columns to support the plants that still evoke a church's nave. Make your way towards it. You will pass Queens Head Passage on your left, which is reputed to have been home to the first chocolate shop in England:

The 'Publick Advertiser' of Tuesday, June 16–22, 1657

In Bishopsgate Street in Queen's Head Alley, at a Frenchman's house, is an excellent West India drink called chocolate, to be sold, where you may have it ready at any time, and also unmade [i.e. dry, to be mixed at home] at reasonable rates.

Pepys mentions chocolate several times in the Diary but, unlike coffee or tea, not as being much of a novelty.

You should now be facing the garden of the ruined Christchurch Greyfriars. This church owes its ruination to the bombing of 1940 and its name to the 'grey friars', or Franciscans, whose monastery was nearby. There seems to have been something of a tradition here of burying the dead in the robes of a Franciscan to ease their passage into heaven. One of those so served was the French princess Isabella, the 'She-Wolf of France', who married King Edward II in 1308, possibly had him murdered at Berkeley Castle in 1327, became regent until 1330, and died in 1358. If so, the trick doesn't seem to have worked; Isabella's ghost is reported to have been seen many times by those heading in for the early shift at St Bartholomew's Hospital. And there is also a connection to Samuel Pepys. Christ's Hospital School was originally based here, having been set up by Edward VI for orphaned children, and in 1673 Pepys persuaded Charles II to set up a Royal Mathematical School to teach navigation (for centuries a matter of exacting calculations) to the boys of Christ's Hospital School and thus prepare them for naval careers. Pepys was later made a governor of the school, and in 1699 he was awarded the Freedom of the City of London partly in recognition of his services to it.

Now, continue up Newgate Street and past the Central Criminal Court which, appropriately enough, covers the old site of London's feared Newgate Prison. Conditions inside Newgate were so appalling that sending a felon here must have saved on many an execution. On 9 May 1667, returning home, Pepys discovered

> in our street, at the Three Tuns' Tavern door, I find a great
> hubbub; and what was it but two brothers have fallen out,
> and one killed the other. And who should they be but the
> two Fieldings [sic]; one whereof, Bazill, was page to my Lady
> Sandwich; and he hath killed the other, himself being very
> drunk, and so is sent to Newgate.

In fact, it was Christopher who had stabbed Basil. The two were the sons of George Feilding, Earl of Desmond, and thus would have been great uncles to Henry Fielding (the spelling seems to have evolved), the author of *Tom Jones* (1749), whose hero Tom is himself hauled off to Newgate after duelling with Mr Fitzpatrick.

At the junction with Old Bailey, turn right into Giltspur Street, passing on your left the church of St Sepulchre-without-Newgate ('without' in this case meaning 'standing outside of', the opposite of 'within'). This is the Old Bailey church, whose bells demand 'When will you pay me?' in the 'Oranges and Lemons' rhyme and which were also tolled as the condemned were led from the prison to execution at Tyburn, out near what is now Marble Arch. It is the burial place of Captain John Smith, one of the founders of Jamestown and the first settlements in Virginia, whose life was supposedly saved by Pocahontas and whom we will come across again later.

If you carry on up Giltspur Street, you will come to another statue of a small boy, the Golden Boy of Pye Corner. Will Hewer's mother lived close by and lost her house in the Great Fire – which was rather bad luck, as the statue of the Golden Boy marks where the northern edge of the Fire burned itself out. Just as now, such a tragedy occasioned any number of crackpot theories to account for it, including French secret agents, Dutch fifth columnists and, as the inscription below the boy states, the 'sin of gluttony'. The lower inscription records the connection of this area with grave robbing, which makes a grim sort of sense with St Bartholomew's Hospital being so close by and there being only one way surgeons acquired a knowledge of anatomy. Indeed, St Sepulchre had a hut in its church-yard where a watchman could keep an eye out for those intent on digging up the newly dead and selling the cadavers to the hospital.

We are now between St Bartholomew's Hospital and Smithfield Market. On your left is Hosier Lane, the setting of one chapter in an extraordinarily fraught and unhappy time in Pepys's household, occasioned by his affair with his wife's 'companion', Deb Willet. The affair began in October 1668; Deb was eighteen and Samuel thirty-five, so you might say the affair was a seventeenth-century version of a midlife crisis, but Deb does genuinely seem to have stirred some particular tenderness in him (this despite the fact that he was also carrying on with Betty Martin and Mrs Bagwell at the time). Elizabeth caught Samuel and Deb pretty much *in flagrante* in November 1668, in her own house, and of course had Deb dismissed at once, but on 19 April 1669 Sam was still pursuing the poor girl, trying to find out if she were now living with her aunt. He then spotted her walking up Holborn and caught up with her at the end of Hosier Lane:

> I led her into a little blind alehouse within the walls, and there
> she and I alone fell to talk and baiser la and toker su mammailles
> [kissed her and touched her breasts], but she mighty coy, and I
> hope modest ... I did give her in a paper 20s., and we did agree
> para meet again in the Hall at Westminster on Monday next.

His second-to-last thought when he closed his Diary for the final time was of Deb, but somehow his marriage to Elizabeth persisted through it all.

Smithfield itself, now facing you, is fascinating. There has been a meat market here since the fourteenth century, so you have to imagine this area as full of the noise of cattle, sheep, and pigs being 'stampeded' down the lanes and alleys and it stinking, frankly, with all the blood and mess of their slaughter and butchery. It was also a place of human execution, until Tyburn took over: the Scottish freedom fighter William Wallace died here in 1305 (a plaque marks the spot); Wat Tyler, leader of the Peasant's Revolt, was betrayed and done to death here in 1381; so were over 200 Protestant martyrs, burned to death during the reign of Bloody Mary (1553–1558). In the early seventeenth century, the area was notorious as a site of duels and was known as Ruffian's Hall, and of course from 1133 to 1855, when it was suppressed, every 24 August for three days the present Victorian Smithfield Market would have been the site of Bartholomew Fair – the biggest, most riotous, most lawless such gathering in London, if not the whole country.

Carry on anti-clockwise round the circular West Smithfield, past the Wallace Memorial and the entrance to Little Britain, where

John Milton lodged in 1662, and you will come to what looks like a Tudor gatehouse. This is in fact an actual house, a half-timbered Elizabethan top storey over a thirteenth-century arch that marks the original entrance to the church of St Bartholomew the Great. You can't really discuss church and hospital separately; both were founded in 1123 by the same man, Rahere, who is variously described as having been a herald, a cleric, a courtier, and a jester to King Henry I. Stow calls him 'a pleasant witted gentleman' and leaves it at that. A vision during an illness led Rahere to build the church, found the hospital, and, very presciently, to establish St Bartholomew's Fair as well, the proceeds and rents from which helped support the church and hospital for centuries.

The church was originally much larger than it now appears (when you walk down the path to its door, as I encourage you to do now, you are walking down what was the nave), but St Bartholomew the Great is still one of the most pleasing and impressive churches you could ask to find. Its knapped flint outer wall gives it the appearance of a country church, and you find an undisturbed and almost rural peace inside as well – astonishing, when you consider the tumult that lapped about it daily for centuries. It has one of the best surviving Norman interiors in London – solid drum columns, perfectly round arches, rugged stone – yet all on a human scale that seems to rotate around and embrace the visitor. And if you are also struck by déjà vu the moment you enter, that is no doubt because it has figured in movie after movie: from *Four Weddings and a Funeral* to *Avengers: Age of Ultron*. But after withstanding both the Fire and the Blitz, Ultron must have seemed very small beer. Rahere still lies here, in a handsome polychrome tomb, and in the days when the Lady Chapel was a commercial workshop, Benjamin Franklin worked here as a printer.

Walk down Little Britain, then left into Montague Street, and bear right to the Rotunda. (In the Rotunda itself, at the time of writing, you will find the Museum of London, which should be on the bucket list of every visitor to the City and every Londoner too – though be aware that it has a move planned in its future, which might disrupt access for a little while.)

Lord love it, but Aldersgate and the Rotunda is drear, with architecture that (to me) has all the charm of the Barbican just to its east. However, in Easter 1667, Aldersgate had been the scene of high drama, and a sad and cautionary tale which is worth recounting here. Pepys had gone to the Old Bailey to follow the case of Christopher Feilding, and found himself listening to the account of two young boys who, while playing on the open ground at Moorfields, had been approached and subsequently groomed by

> one rogue, Gabriel Holmes, [who] did come to them and teach them to drink, and then to bring him plate and clothes from their fathers' houses, and carry him into their houses, and leaving open the doors for him...

These boys, Pepys noted, were of good families ('it is worth considering how unsafe it is to have children play up and down this lewd town'), and were caught when they set fire to two houses in Aldersgate Street, one to provide a diversion while they stole the goods that had been thrown into the street from the other as it burned. Not only that, but one of them disabled a fire engine by pulling the plug from its reservoir of water; not only that but, seeing the sheriff, Sir Joseph Shelden, at the fire, they tried to set fire to Shelden's house in his absence too. According to Pepys:

the two little boys who did give so good account of particulars that I never heard children in my life. [...] But that which was most remarkable was the impudence of this Holmes, who hath been arraigned often, and still got away; and on this business was taken and broke loose just at Newgate Gate; and was last night luckily taken about Bow, who got loose, and run into the river, and hid himself in the rushes; and they pursued him with a dog, and the dog got him and held him till he was taken.

Good dog! Holmes was no doubt hung, but one wonders what became of the two boys.

On we go – turn south on the Rotunda, down the lower half of Aldersgate Street to St Botolph's without Aldersgate and head on into Postman's Park. This is a purely nineteenth-century creation, the brainchild of the artist G. F. Watts, but such an oddity can't be passed by. The idea was to commemorate acts of heroism by the ordinary folk of London – and so it does, in numerous very beautifully lettered ceramic plaques. But the impulse behind it does rather backfire: the circumstances the plaques record are often so bizarre as to distract from the bravery of what the individuals did. It's very much of a piece with that Victorian taste for sensationalism that gave us the penny dreadful and Sweeney Todd.

Continue down Aldersgate Street and turn left into Gresham Street, then right into Foster Lane, past the Goldsmith's Company Hall. There have always been gold- and silversmiths in this part of the City, one of whom – the silversmith Mary King – created plate for Samuel Pepys. And we know this because one such piece of plate, a silver 'trencher', with her hallmark and his crest, was acquired in October 2019 by the Museum of London. Foster Lane is also home to St Vedast-alias-Foster church, one of the least known in all

London, with its minute garden complete with a section of Roman mosaic found in nearby Friday Street.

We're now working our way back into the old City, and in particular its seventeenth-century commercial and retail centre. This is where you have to recall the buildings of Staple Inn from Walk 1 and, when Foster Lane brings you out on Cheapside, reconstruct it in your imagination as one half-timbered Tudor frontage after another, all of them bustling with stallholders, shopkeepers, pickpockets, and good citizens like Sam. The Cheapside Hoard of jewellery (also now in the Museum of London) was discovered here in 1912, having been buried by its original owner in a rush to either get away from the plague or escape the Great Fire, and so lost. As well as shops, there was a public pillory and, this being London, taverns and churches alternating all the way along Cheapside's not inconsiderable length as it becomes first Cornhill and then Leadenhall Street – all retail thoroughfares, as was Cannon Street to the south, parallel to both Cheapside and the river Thames, from which one has to imagine goods and new stock being ferried continually. Very different to the grey-suited quiet of this part of the City now, which only ever seems to be alive for the morning and evening rush-hours – and at lunchtime.

One of Cheapside's churches is St Mary-le-Bow, appearing on your right; step now into its churchyard, where a large tree stands. Pepys was born within ear's reach of St Mary-le-Bow's bells (in the seventeenth century, at least; they carry much less far amongst the noise of London today), so would have qualified as a cockney without doubt. The original church was another casualty of the Fire, and what we see now is another Wren church. Wren's spire has always been particularly admired, as has the dragon weathervane at its top, which was once scaled by the acrobat Jacob Hall, whom Pepys saw tightrope walking in Southwark (see Walk 3). Captain John Smith, who lies at St-Sepulchre-without-Newgate and who had a life full of enough incident to fill at least five, was a parishioner here, hence his statue being beside the church. Leave him on your right and disappear round the back of the church onto Bow Lane. Turn right and you will find Williamson's Tavern, which occupies what was once the site of the house of Sir John Fastolf (immortalised by Shakespeare as 'Falstaff') and which also served as the Lord Mayor's house from 1670 to 1753. It has been Williamson's Tavern ever since. Continue out into Watling Street, with Ye Olde Watling pub facing you.

Watling Street is indeed old. Its name is said to come from that of the Waeclingas tribe, who were once to be found out near St Albans, and the street itself is a part of the Roman route from St Albans to Dover. Ye Olde Watling pub was newly built three months before the Fire took it; Pepys, standing here aghast on 2 September 1666, recorded being surrounded by 'every creature coming away laden with goods to save, and here and there sicke people carried away in beds. Extraordinary good goods [sic], carried in carts and on backs.' Imagine the sounds of the Fire and the glow in the sky, with the old square tower of St Paul's outlined against it, the air full of smoke and embers, and the noise coming up from the river of people crowding into any boat they could find. As London was rebuilt, this pub became an office for Wren's team and a refuelling spot for his workmen.

Turn left and walk to the end of Watling Street, then turn left up Queen Victoria Street and go on up to Bank. On your left is a shopping mall with a striped façade and, running through it, Bucklersbury Passage. Pepys was here on 13 June 1663: 'Thence by coach, with a mad coachman, that drove like mad, and down byeways, through Bucklersbury home, everybody through the street cursing him, being ready to run over them.' It leads back onto Cheapside, at the point where technically it becomes Poultry, named for – you guessed it – selling birds (the 'Chepe' in Cheapside, by the way, simply meant 'market' in Old English, rather than hinting at the quality of goods sold there). As well as the sale of poultry, this street was well known for the number of taverns it could boast and for the street Old Jewry, to be found just above it to the north. London's Jewish community, banished from the country since 1290, was just beginning to re-establish itself in Pepys's time, having been allowed to return in 1657 during the Protectorate. The original medieval synagogue had been here.

But let us push on eastward, in this case up Threadneedle Street from Bank toward Merchant Taylors' Hall. The Merchant Taylors have been here since 1347, and it is the association with tailoring that of course gives the street its name. We, however, will pause at Finch Lane before reaching Merchant Taylors' Hall, and take this back down to Cornhill, where we will locate Ball Court, just to the east of Birchin Lane, because here is another bit of time travel for you that is too good to miss. Enter Ball Court, and you will encounter firstly Simpson's Tavern, which was created out of two seventeenth-century houses in 1757, and secondly the George and Vulture public house, famous for its associations with Charles Dickens and *The Pickwick Papers*; it is here that Mr Pickwick and Sam Weller lodge, and where Mr Pickwick is had up for breach of promise. It was originally an old coaching inn for those travelling on to Essex. And just around the corner in St Michael's Alley is what Pepys refers to as 'the Coffee House in Cornhill'. This, now the Jamaica Wine House, was the first coffee-house in London, and Pepys was here on 10 December 1660:

in the evening to the Coffee House in Cornhill, the first time
that ever I was there, and I found much pleasure in it, through
the diversity of company and discourse.

Pasqua Rosée, who may have come from either Armenia or Lebanon,
opened his coffee-house here in 1652. By the eighteenth century, it
had become a particular haunt for merchants in the unholy trade
with the Caribbean in enslaved people and sugar, hence its present
name. It, like Simpson's, has a dark and cluttered and highly atmos-
pheric interior, which doesn't quite date back to Pepys's day but is
still old enough to leave you blinking as you re-emerge into the light
of twenty-first century London. Seventeenth-century coffee, by the
way, was served cold, in thimble-sized cups, and scented with rose
water to make it less bitter and unappealing. The effect of caffeine
upon the seventeenth-century brain has been held responsible for
the creation of the Royal Society and the foundation of modern
science. The truth we will never know.

Take yourself further down St Michael's Alley and turn right,
through a covered passageway, into Bell Inn Yard. Turning left
will then bring you out onto Gracechurch Street. Two of the most
poignant moments in the Diary happen here. The first is when, on
3 September 1665, Pepys is listening to the news from the plague-
ravaged City:

Among other stories, one was very passionate, methought, of
a complaint brought against a man in the towne for taking a
child from London from an infected house. Alderman Hooker
told us it was the child of a very able citizen in Gracious
[Gracechurch] Street, a saddler, who had buried all the rest of
his children of the plague, and himself and wife now being shut

up and in despair of escaping, did desire only to save the life of this little child; and so prevailed to have it received stark-naked into the arms of a friend, who brought it (having put it into new fresh clothes) to Greenwich; where upon hearing the story, we did agree it should be permitted to be received and kept in the towne.

The second is when he is quite overcome by the losses all about him, writing on 14 September of

meeting dead corpses of the plague, carried to be buried close to me at noon-day through the City in Fanchurch-street. To see a person sick of the sores, carried close by me by Gracechurch in a hackney-coach. My finding the Angell tavern, at the lower end of Tower-hill, shut up, and more than that, the alehouse at the Tower-stairs, and more than that, the person was then dying of the plague when I was last there, a little while ago, at night, to write a short letter there, and I overheard the mistresse of the house sadly saying to her husband somebody was very ill, but did not think it was of the plague. To hear that poor Payne, my waiter, hath buried a child, and is dying himself. To hear that a labourer I sent but the other day to Dagenhams, to know how they did there, is dead of the plague; and that one of my own watermen, that carried me daily, fell sick as soon as he had landed me on Friday morning last, when I had been all night upon the water... and is now dead of the plague. To hear that Mr. Lewes hath another daughter sick. And, lastly, that both my servants, W. Hewer and Tom Edwards, have lost their fathers, both in St Sepulchre's parish, of the plague this week, do put me into great apprehensions of melancholy, and with good reason.

No one had a clue what caused the plague in 1665 or how it was spread; all one could do was absent oneself, as Pepys did, taking lodgings down in Greenwich for himself and in Woolwich for Elizabeth (see Walk 4), but even so he had some narrow escapes. It's been suggested that some people had a measure of natural immunity to the bacterium that caused the plague; if so, Samuel might well have been one of them.

We are now heading toward Seething Lane and Samuel's home turf. Walk south down Gracechurch Street, then east along Fenchurch Street, passing Lime Street on your left, where on 21 January 1664 Pepys saw one 'Turner' hung for robbery: 'flung off the ladder in his cloake. A comely-looked man he was, and kept his countenance to the end' (this street is also where, on the corner with Fenchurch Street, Ebenezer Scrooge's house was situated – at least in Charles Dickens's imagination). On your right, you will also pass Philpot Lane (where the Pepyses were guests at a wedding on 8 August 1666: 'A good-dinner, and, what was best, good musique') and, after two more blocks, Mincing Lane. The culinary-sounding names here are particularly misleading, neither of them having anything to do with mincing or seething as we understand them. 'Mincing' is a corruption of 'mynchen', another name for a nun, while 'seething' is an old term for grain that has yet to be threshed. So the one refers to the good sisters of the Benedictine nunnery of nearby St Helen's Bishopsgate, and the other to the processing of grain, perhaps here in the street, before it was sold on medieval Cornhill.

Turn down Mincing Lane, and left into Dunster Court, where the Worshipful Company of Clothworkers – who made Samuel Pepys, son of the tailor John Pepys, their Master in 1677 – have their hall (Samuel presented them with a magnificent silver cup, which the Clothworkers still have). Turn right onto Mark Lane, then left into Hart Street. In Pepys's day, you would now be standing in front of one of old London's strangest buildings – Whittington's Palace – which stood here possibly from the days of Henry VIII until 1801. The entire front of the house, which made up three sides of a square, was extravagantly carved timber, with the two sides at left and right almost entirely lattice windows. Every other surface was decorated with the carved heads of cats, wild beasts, goblins, and armorial shields. The connection with Whittington seems to have been another of those dreamed up by later imaginative Londoners. From descriptions of its location, it sounds as if it might have stood roughly where the Ship public house stands now – so Pepys's church of St Olave's would have been its neighbour.

St Olave's is still with us in part because, urged on by Sir William Penn on the worst night of the Fire, the workmen from the local navy yards and the garrison at the Tower were so energetic in pulling down houses to create a firebreak, which stopped the flames between Mincing Lane and Mark Lane. Pepys was extraordinarily lucky here: the three streets in his neighbourhood – Mincing Lane, Mark Lane, and Seething Lane itself – run side by side, down towards what is now Lower Thames Street and the river, and on John Leake's engraved map of 1667, the *Survey of the City after the Great Fire*, you can see that Mincing Lane would have been nothing but ash and that the edge of the Fire reached as close as the houses on the east side of Mark Lane before the wind changed direction. It was this happy chance that saved St Dunstan's, Smithfield, and Seething Lane.

St Olave's is a tiny little building, one of the many that make you marvel at how much London can squeeze into the smallest footprint, and for this reason it was beloved by Sir John Betjeman and also by Dickens, who seems to have been particularly taken by its gateway with the five carved skulls, and who in his *Uncommercial Traveller* christened it, rather unfairly, 'St Ghastly Grim'. Turn right into Seething Lane to see the impressive tulip tree in its tiny grave-yard, shading the front of the church and making a burst of green in this small shadowy street, with flowers like chalices of amethyst enamel – and notice how much higher the ground in the church-yard is than the door to the church. The ground rose as the plague victims in the parish were buried here; this graceful tree is what they have become.

The interior of St Olave's is a delight. Three huge arches march down either side of the aisle, as if expecting to find themselves in a much larger building, and come to a startled halt at the altar. Eliza-beth Pepys, bossy and interrogative, looks down from her memorial high above the altar on the left; Pepys himself is on the right-hand wall, and the rest of the church is full of memorials to honest striv-ers and boys-made-good from the Tudor period to the eighteenth century. It seems eminently suitable that Pepys should rest here.

Pepys's own house was pretty much on the site where the Four Seasons Hotel now stands, with its plaque and bust of Sam. Make your way down the road towards it now. His was one of a square of dwelling houses built around the Navy Office itself, so when Pepys talks of travelling 'to my office', his commute was enviably short. Each house had three storeys plus an attic, and the Navy Office itself – in our one surviving image of it – looks brick-built with smart stonework corners and doorway, and steps up to the door. Sadly, the proximity of office and houses meant that when in 1673 a care-less hand left a candle burning unattended at the home of that other navy man Lord Brouncker, the Navy Office and the houses round it all went up together. It was said that the blaze began in the apart-ment of Brouncker's mistress, Abigail Williams – a maidservant was supposed to have been to blame, but I think from Pepys's dealings with Abigail (see Walk 3) we can guess whom he would have held responsible. After the fire, Pepys initially moved into lodgings in Hart Street, but it cannot have been the same.

The Three Tuns, scene of that tragic falling-out between the Feilding brothers, was at the top end of Seething Lane, where it becomes Crutched Friars – another misleading name, as the friars had nothing to do with crutches but were instead 'cruciferi', or of the cross. Muscovy Street, at the bottom of Seething Lane, is so named after another public house, the Czar of Muscovy, which used to stand there and is meant to have been a favourite with Peter the Great when he visited London as part of his 'Grand Embassy' of 1697–1698. There is more of Peter the Great to come when we explore the other side of the river down to Greenwich, but that is Walk 4. Having travelled, on Walks 1 and 2, all the way through Samuel Pepys's professional life, you may choose to rest your legs inside the Four Seasons Hotel, or in contemplating its little garden. Or, if you feel the urge to continue, you may skip ahead to Walk 5 and, following it from page 123, carry on in Sam's footsteps all the way along the north bank of the river to Wapping. If none of those appeals, never fear. In Walk 3, we will go shamelessly in search of entertainment.

WALK 3

A Night Out with Mr Pepys

THIS WALK IS DESIGNED to bring out your inner *flâneur*. We all have one – the ambulant observer, the traveller through the streets, interested in everything but halted by very little. The crowd flows round us, on its way, but those others in it are working – we are at leisure. London, for the *flâneur*, is like a toy theatre, where one engaging scene succeeds another and we let them roll toward us, at our ease.

This is another half-day walk of about seven kilometres or so, depending on how many times you break step with your inner *flâneur* and dart back as something too good not to investigate catches your eye. It will take you from St James's Park into Covent Garden, to Lincoln's Inn Fields, and down to the Middle Temple, then along the river, over Blackfriars Bridge and into Southwark, from the highly fashionable to the demi-mondaine – or worse. On the way, it will take you into taverns, theatres, brothels, a mighty coaching inn, and one of the saddest and most affecting graveyards in all of London – old even in the time of Samuel Pepys.

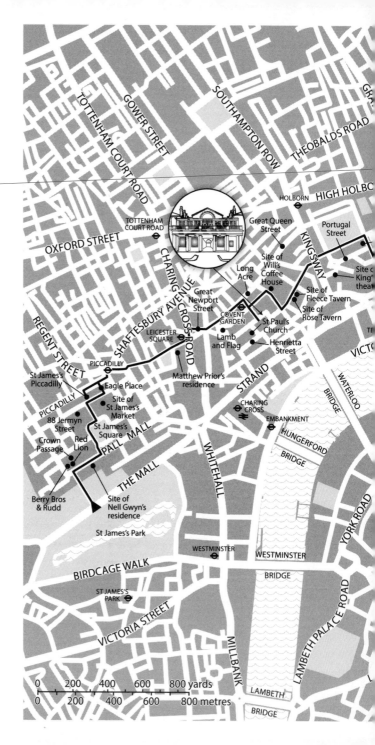

TOTTENHAM COURT ROAD

GOWER STREET

SOUTHAMPTON ROW

THEOBALDS ROAD

GRA

HOLBORN

HIGH HOLBO

TOTTENHAM COURT ROAD

Great Queen Street

Portugal Street

OXFORD STREET

CHARING CROSS ROAD

Long Acre

Site of Will's Coffee House

KINGSWAY

Site of King' thea

Great Newport Street

Site of Fleece Tavern

SHAFTESBURY AVENUE

COVENT GARDEN

St Paul's Church

Site of Rose Tavern

TE

VICT

REGENT STREET

LEICESTER SQUARE

Lamb and Flag

Henrietta Street

WATERLOO

BRIDGE

PICCADILLY

Matthew Prior's residence

STRAND

St James's Piccadilly

Eagle Place

PICCADILLY

Site of St James's Market

CHARING CROSS

EMBANKMENT

88 Jermyn Street

St James's Square

HUNGERFORD

BRIDGE

Crown Passage

Red Lion

PALL MALL

WHITEHALL

Berry Bros & Rudd

THE MALL

YORK ROAD

Site of Nell Gwyn's residence

St James's Park

WESTMINSTER

WESTMINSTER

BRIDGE

BIRDCAGE WALK

ST JAMES'S PARK

LAMBETH PALACE ROAD

VICTORIA STREET

MILLBANK

0   200   400   600   800 yards
0   200   400   600   800 metres

LAMBETH

BRIDGE

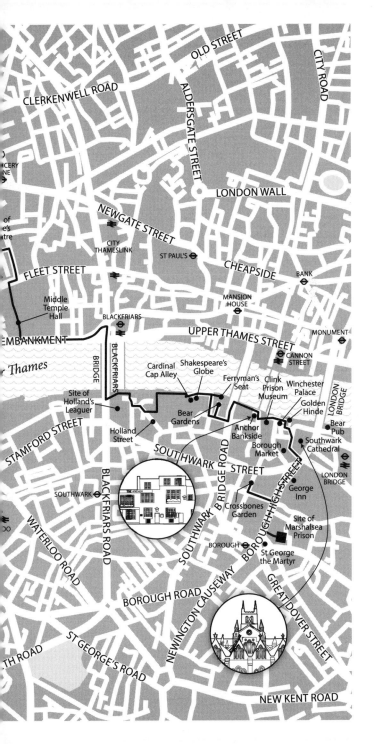

Our ideas today of a good night out, and Sam's, would I think be found to be very similar if examined side by side, but there would be a few important differences of which you should be aware. First of all, timings have shifted. Sam was an early riser, up and doing many mornings before it was even light (though he could be a night owl too – 17 February 1664, for example, finds him in his office addressing us at 4am 'all alone, cold, and my candle not enough left to light me to my owne house'), but for most people, sunrise and sunset marked the beginning and end of the day. Shops would shut as soon as it grew dark, for example. Theatres, where Sam went as often as he could, opened their doors in the afternoon and shut them at six, so supper would most definitely come after the show (the main meal of the day was taken at lunchtime – this is the one Sam means when he writes 'dinner'). If you slipped in for the last two acts of a play, you could watch without paying; if you didn't think much of the show, you could leave at the end of the first act and no one would expect you to pay either– the theatrical equivalent of Kindle's 'Try a sample' – so the 150 or so different productions mentioned in the Diary were by no means watched all the way through. And in Restoration London, the long run in the theatre was unknown; a new production opened every few days. There were nine theatres active in London at the time, from the rowdy Red Bull up in Clerkenwell to that in Salisbury Court, a mere step from Sam's childhood home. The most important were, first, the Duke's House (the duke being James, Duke of York, brother to the king) in what had been Lisle's Tennis Court in Portugal Street below Lincoln's Inn Fields, and, second, the King's House, which also started life in 1660 in an old tennis court, near to Clare Market, again below Lincoln's Inn Fields, but then moved in 1663 to Drury Lane and became what is now the Theatre Royal. Otherwise, Sam's idea of a 'mighty merry' evening and ours would be much the same – good food, good wine, good company, good entertainment, some gossip, some scandal, seeing and (once arrayed, obviously, in one's best) being seen.

We'll begin in St James's Park, somewhere with a view of the lake, perhaps, because along with all the fashionable pleasures of the times there was what we might call now *la passeggiata* – the stroll – and if you were going to stroll, St James's Park was a very good place in which to do it. First of all, you were bound to encounter members of the court there, if not of the royal family itself, strolling over from Whitehall Palace. And where the court led, all fashionable London would follow – even if some of the goings-on in this 'all sin-sheltering grove', as John Wilmot, Earl of Rochester, described it, were best not spied upon too closely, especially once dusk had fallen (and Rochester would have known, if anyone did). The park was also a good place to do business: Sir William Coventry, for example, another high-up in the administration of the navy, was often to be encountered here. And there was always something new to admire in your surroundings. Pepys was much struck by the 'brave alterations' Charles II had made to St James's Park in September 1661 after bringing the garden designer André Mollet over from Versailles to knock the place into shape. Pepys saw his first orange trees here in April 1664, and on the new canal, now St James's Park Lake, the 'great variety of fowl' that still delight Londoners today, including no doubt the pelicans, the first of which were a gift from the Russian Ambassador in 1664. (The Ambassador was probably glad to be rid of them – I have seen a St James's Park pelican help itself to a live pigeon, whole, from beside the patch of grass on which it had been taking its ease, gulp it down, and settle back again with as little concern as if all it had done were burp.) However, it was unwise to be too *à la mode* in public. Here is Pepys opening his heart to his Diary on 10 May 1669; first he is told by his professional rival, John Creed, that his new coach and horses have excited the wrong sort of comment, as being too 'fine', and then his dress is criticised as too showy:

> Povy [Thomas Povey, a London merchant] told me of my gold-lace sleeves in the Park yesterday, which vexed me also, so as to resolve never to appear in Court with them, but presently to have them taken off, as it is fit I should, and so to my wife at Unthanke's [sic; Elizabeth's tailor, in Charing Cross], and coach, and so called at my tailor's to that purpose, and so home, and after a little walk in the garden, home to supper and to bed.

Come out of the park, cross over The Mall, and walk up Marlborough Road. On your left is St James's Palace, which became the centre of the court in London after Whitehall had burned down. Note in particular the red-brick Tudor gatehouse: first because its two towers remind one so unmistakably of the two gouty legs of Henry VIII, who began building here in 1531, and second because there were two more tower gatehouses like this across King Street in Westminster. In a room at the top of one of these, Samuel and his new bride (who, shockingly to us, was just shy of her fifteenth birthday) had set up home in the winter of 1655. Now here he was, the tailor's boy from Fleet Street, with a house in the City; moneyed, successful, professionally of immense account, strolling across St James's Park with gold lace on his sleeves, and perfectly likely to have James, Duke of York and Lord High Admiral, greet him by name. I'll bet Creed and Povey were viridian with envy.

You will now reach Pall Mall, which was also laid out by Charles II, so that he could have somewhere to play 'pall-mall' (a forerunner of croquet) without coaches driving past him and raising up clouds of dust as he played. Ahead of you over the road you will see another of London's intriguing little alleyways. This is Crown Passage, and it gives you an excellent idea of how narrow a typical London street might have been. On its left-hand side is the Red Lion pub, which claims to be one of the oldest in London and, if they let you see it, has a venerable panelled parlour on its first floor. If you like, make a small detour here to St James's Street, where you will see Berry Bros & Rudd, wine merchants, who claim to have been here since 1698. Otherwise, head eastward – passing Number 79 Pall Mall, where Charles II installed Nell Gwyn once her orange-selling days were behind her – and then turn left into St James's Square. This area was open fields until at least 1661, but twenty years later it was being developed into one of the most fashionable addresses in London. E. V. Lucas, in his 1909 book *A Wanderer in London*, calls St James's Street and Pall Mall 'the principal male streets of London', with their one club after another: Whites, the Oxford and Cambridge, the Reform, the Army and Navy, the Carlton... 'Secular, sombre, and silent monasteries' was how Lucas thought of them. Strange to think that they had their beginnings in the coffee- and chocolate-houses of St James's Street, with their wits and rakes, embryonic Whig and Tory parties, and ferocious, noisy debate over the news of the day.

Henry Jermyn, 1st Earl of St Albans, was behind the development of St James's and thus set an example for the development of the whole of the West End. Jermyn (as in Jermyn Street) was a Royalist so deeply dyed that he was rumoured to have secretly married Charles I's queen, Henrietta Maria, after Charles's execution. Before Charles II granted permission to develop the area, St James's was chiefly known for its fair, which lasted for a week after St James's

Day in July and was every bit as riotous as St Bartholomew's Fair up in Smithfield. As well as developing St James's Square and the streets around it, Jermyn moved the fair into a specially built market house in the area just north of the square itself, where it became a much more sedate affair. Pepys came here in pursuit of art in April 1669:

> to Loton, the landscape-drawer, a Dutchman, living in
> St. James's Market, but there saw no good pictures. But by
> accident he did direct us to a painter that was then in the house
> with him, a Dutchman, newly come over, one Evarelst [Simon
> Verelst], who took us to his lodging close by, and did shew us a
> little flower-pot of his doing, the finest thing that ever, I think,
> I saw in my life; the drops of dew hanging on the leaves, so
> as I was forced, again and again, to put my finger to it, to feel
> whether my eyes were deceived or no. He do ask 70*l*. for it: I
> had the vanity to bid him 20*l*.; but a better picture I never saw
> in my whole life; and it is worth going twenty miles to see it.

On 12 April he again offered Verelst twenty pounds for his 'flower pot', but Verelst (who called himself 'the God of Flowers') still wanted more than double that. Just as now, St James's was not a place to shop or live unless one had deep pockets, or were the very good friend of someone who had. James II kept his mistress Catherine Sedley in St James's Square; Moll Davis, dancer and one-time mistress to his brother Charles II, did well enough out of this association (much to the fury of Nell Gwyn) to buy her own house on the square in 1673. One of the few moments in the Diary when we hear Elizabeth Pepys speak is when she describes Moll as 'the most impertinent slut in the world', after viewing Moll's behaviour in the audience at the Duke's House theatre in Lincoln's Inn Fields.

Head north out of St James's Square, up Duke of York Street to Jermyn Street, and then along Jermyn Street to Eagle Place. In the 1680s, Verelst himself (according to Peter Cunningham's *Handbook of London*) was living in Eagle Place, and was thus near neighbour to Frances Stuart, 'La Belle Stuart', who sat as the original model for the figure of Britannia found on pre-decimal British currency. Pepys thought Frances was the most beautiful woman he had ever seen 'with her sweet eye, little Roman nose, and excellent taille [waist]', ousting even Barbara Villiers in his opinion (and supposedly in Charles II's as well), and he was distraught when he heard in March 1668 that she had contracted smallpox.

Eagle Place will take you out onto Piccadilly, and since no fashionable new neighbourhood would have been complete without its church, walk back along Piccadilly a very few yards to explore St James's Piccadilly. This is yet another London church designed by Wren, and it is one of which he was reputedly very proud. It has a reredos and font carved by Grinling Gibbons, no less, and has been something of a trailblazer in the Anglican church: an early supporter of the ordination of women and of rights for the LGBTQ+ community and for asylum seekers. REM have played here, and there have been notable political sculpture installations in its grounds. It hosts a pretty little market, too, the historical shade of St James's Fair.

Piccadilly is supposed to have been named after a local manufacturer of piccadills – those broad, flat collars, like an opened book, seen framing the face in so many Jacobean portraits. Walk east along Piccadilly to the statue of Eros. If you wish to be picky, you may now point out to any walking companion that the statue is technically of 'Anteros', god of requited love, rather than of Eros, who is the god of sex and erotic pleasure. Whatever (as your companion may well reply) or whoever the statue, it also marks the site of what looks in the Faithorne and Newcourt map of 1658 to have been a sizeable gaming house: two storeys, plus attic, with a walled area of some sort to the side, and open to the sky in the same way as the theatres of the day. With such entertainment in mind, go round Eros/Anteros and down Coventry Street to Leicester Square. In 1846, the biographer and historian J. T. Smith, in his *An Antiquarian Ramble in the Streets of London*, was complaining of the number of gaming houses still in the neighbourhood, claiming 'the bad character of the place was at least two centuries old'. Pepys, with his cautious tradesman's blood, was baffled by the mania for gambling that possessed so many of his peers, and it most definitely did not figure in his notion of an evening's entertainment. Watching a cockfight in Shoe Lane off Fleet Street in December 1663, he wrote censoriously:

> Lord! to see the strange variety of people, from Parliament-man (by name Wildes, that was Deputy Governor of the Tower when Robinson was Lord Mayor) to the poorest 'prentices, bakers, brewers, butchers, draymen, and what not; and all these fellows one with another in swearing, cursing, and betting... One thing more it is strange to see how people of this poor rank, that look as if they had not bread to put in their mouths, shall bet three or four pounds at one bet, and lose it, and yet bet as much the next battle (so they call every match of two cocks), so that one of them will lose 10*l.* or 20*l.* at a meeting.

But yet they still do.

The land on which now lies Leicester Square belonged to the Sidney family, earls of Leicester, who built their enormous London mansion on its north side and, to the south, laid out streets and houses in the 1670s 'for the good and benefit of the family... and the decency of the place before Leicester House'. At that date this was a properly respectable neighbourhood; the poet Matthew Prior (1664–1721) lived at Number 21. On one of Verelst's 'flower pots' Prior penned:

> When fam'd Varelst this little Wonder drew
> Flora vouchsaf'd the growing Work to view.
> Finding the Painter's Science at a Stand,
> The Goddess snatch'd the Pencil from his Hand,
> And finishing the Piece, She smiling said;
> Behold One Work of Mine, that ne'er shall fade.

Later denizens of the square included William Hogarth and Joshua Reynolds. Lord knows what they would make of it now.

And now we are coming up to another of Restoration London's new and fashionable neighbourhoods: Covent Garden. Continue from Leicester Square onto Cranbourn Street, turn left up Charing Cross Road and cross over onto Great Newport Street, where Sam's well-to-do cousin Tom was living at one point, then up to Long Acre, where Cromwell lodged from 1637 to 1643, where the poet and critic John Dryden had the lease of an inn – the Mourning Dove – from 1645 to 1653, and where Pepys's father-in-law was living 'among all the whore houses' in 1663. And there was a fashionable coachmakers here, too. All those long hours in his office had paid off: at the end of April 1669, Pepys was supervising the finishing touches being put to a carriage of his very own, the same one that would so excite Creed's spite:

> ... I to my coach-maker's, and there vexed to see nothing yet
> done to my coach, at three in the afternoon; but I set it in doing,

and stood by it till eight at night, and saw the painter varnish
which is pretty to see how every doing it over do make it more
and more yellow; and it dries as fast in the sun as it can be laid
on almost; and most coaches are, now-a-days done so, and it is
very pretty when laid on well...

Covent Garden had been laid out from 1630 at the behest of the
Bedfords by Inigo Jones, in the Italian style that at the time baffled
many Londoners. Faithorne and Newcourt seem unable even to get
their cartographic tongues round the vocabulary for this new phenomenon, labelling its centre the 'Piatze'. So now turn right down
James Street, and the Piazza as it is today will be before you. The
area would never attain the aristocratic respectability of St James's.
First of all there was the famous market, to keep it rough around the
edges; then there were the brothels and taverns (including today's
Lamb and Flag, in whose alley in 1679 John Dryden was beaten up
by a gang of thugs hired by the Earl of Rochester in a poetical spat
gone very wrong indeed). And then there were all those actors and
actresses who had made the area their own, including Thomas Killigrew, who began as a stagehand at the Red Bull up in Clerkenwell,
who was as close as the court of Charles II came to having a jester,
and who ran the new King's House theatre in Drury Lane from
1663, which had Pepys's own Mrs Knepp in its company.

Pepys openly admired Elizabeth Knepp to a degree that for a
married man was both unwise and unfair, although you have to say
that in many places in the Diary she sounds likely to have made a
better fit as a partner for him than the other Elizabeth, his wife.
Whether he would have been as good a fit for her is another question. Mrs Knepp (or Knipp, the spelling is mutable) specialised in
the kind of tough, sexually liberated female characters for which

Restoration comedy is famous, and she seems to have been much like that in real life too. Pepys relished her conversation, they both loved music and singing, and he was very struck by her skill on stage, describing how, in *The Duke of Lerma* at the King's House in February 1668, she 'spoke beyond any creature I ever heard'. He was forever ducking into the theatre on the off-chance he would find her on one side of the footlights or the other, and hanging around the Piazza in the hope she would appear. (She also took Pepys backstage at the King's House, where he saw Nell Gwyn undressed.) Often, he seems to have chosen her company over that of his wife, as on the evening of 6 August 1666 when he, Mrs Knepp, and Mr and Mrs James Pearse left a jealous Mrs Pepys at home 'in chagrin humour' and Sam took everyone else out to dinner:

> I took them to Old Fish Streete, to the very house and woman where I kept my wedding dinner, where I never was since, and there I did give them a jole [tail] of salmon, and what else was to be had. And here we talked of the ill-humour of my wife, which I did excuse as much as I could, and they seemed to admit of it, but did both confess they wondered at it; but from thence to other discourse, and among others to that of my Lord Bruncker [Brouncker] and Mrs. Williams...

William Brouncker, 2nd Viscount Brouncker, was Commissioner of the Navy and his mistress, Abigail Williams, was another actress. Abigail, however, was also a Cromwell by marriage and a member of the gentry by birth, so when Pepys dared call her 'a mad jade' (as he might have done Knepp) she put him in his place. After that, no bad thing he heard of Mrs Williams could be bad enough. At that same dinner in Old Fish Street, Knepp delighted him with gossip that my Lord keeps another woman besides Mrs. Williams; and that, when I was there the other day, there was a great hubbub in the house, Mrs. Williams being fallen sicke, because my Lord was gone to his other mistresse, making her wait for him, till his return from the other mistresse; and a great deale of do there was about it; and Mrs. Williams swounded at it.

Perhaps Abigail Williams's profession helps explain why Lord Brouncker also had a house in Covent Garden. The stage community bridged the divide in this area between high society and low. By way of example, St Paul's Church (to the left of the Piazza, if you care to make another little detour), the 'actor's church' in Covent Garden, is also the resting place of one of the first highwaymen, the dashing Frenchman Claude Duval, who was finally arrested, possibly in Chandos Street in Covent Garden or perhaps where the Coal Hole is now in the Strand, and hanged at Tyburn on 21 January 1670. Pepys was in the crowd. Highway robbery, however, was as nothing compared to some of the goings-on in Covent Garden, as on 1 July 1663:

Mr. Batten telling us of a late triall of Sir Charles Sydly the other day, before my Lord Chief Justice Foster and the whole bench, for his debauchery a little while since at Oxford Kate's, coming in open day into the Balcone and showed his nakedness, ... and abusing of scripture and as it were from thence preaching a mountebank sermon from the pulpit, saying that there he had to sell such a powder as should make all the [women] in town run after him...

Oxford Kate's was the Cock Tavern in Bow Street, and Bow Street is where you should go next, back up James Street, turning right onto Floral Street and right again at its end. Also on Bow Street, at Number 1, was Will's Coffee House, the domain in Pepys's day of John Dryden and later patronised by Alexander Pope, Jonathan Swift, and Dr Johnson, among many other notables.

> I stopped at the great Coffee-house there [Pepys writes in February 1664], where I never was before; where Dryden the poet (I knew at Cambridge), and all the wits of the town, and [Henry] Harris the player, and Mr. Hoole of our College. And had I had time then, or could at other times, it will be good coming thither, for there, I perceive, is very witty and pleasant discourse.

At the end of Bow Street, turn right onto Russell Street. Here, in Samuel's day, you would find the Rose Tavern, where, in 1660, Pepys first sampled *aqua vitae* (which could at the time refer to any number of distilled spirits and which put him 'out of order'). The Rose would have a starring role in the next century in Hogarth's *A Rake's Progress* as the setting for *The Orgy* tavern scene. Next door to the Rose was the Fleece, where in 1661 Pepys and Clement Sankey, later to be Rector of St Clement Eastcheap (the rival 'Oranges and Lemons' church), attempted to take one Mary Archer, a country lass from Cambridge, for a nightcap.

> [But] Mr. Sanchy could not by any argument get his lady to trust herself with him into the tavern, which he was much troubled at, and so we returned immediately into the city by coach, and at the Mitre in Cheapside there light and drank, and then set her at her uncle's in the Old Jewry.

Clement and Mary would eventually marry in 1669, but she was absolutely right not to set foot in the Fleece. 'Very unfortunate for homicides' was John Aubrey's verdict upon it. It's rather a relief after all this drama to record that Covent Garden was where Pepys saw as safe an entertainment as the first Punch and Judy show in England (also recorded on a plaque in the actor's church), on 9 May 1662: 'an Italian puppet play ... very pretty, the best that ever I saw, and great resort of gallants'.

The other great theatre in London was the Duke's House, which is where we shall now make our way – up Kemble Street and over Kingsway to Lincoln's Inn Fields, via Sardinia Street. The Duke's House was on the south side of the Fields, close to Serle Street. Pepys was at a performance here of *Heraclius*, a crazily overblown tragedy by Pierre Corneille, on 5 September 1667 with his neighbour Mary Batelier, Sir William Penn (father of the founder of Pennsylvania), and Elizabeth. This time it was Sam who was in chagrin humour. First of all, his companions were rowdy enough to spoil the play for him, and then 'my wife was ill, and so I was forced to go out of the house with her to Lincoln's Inn walks, and there in a corner she did her business' – thus there is some corner of Lincoln's Inn Fields that is forever Mrs Pepys.

Lincoln's Inn Fields was also being developed at this time, with smart new town houses lining up around the open fields (Povey, who made a good living out of being utterly incompetent, had one of them on the west side). Now is our opportunity to swap from the Faithorne and Newcourt map of 1658 to that of John Ogilby and William Morgan of 1676 – which is the first to present the city not in charming (if unreliable) old-fashioned perspective but with the much more modern-looking exact footprint of the buildings and streets. In it, Bell Yard, from Walk 1, can be seen running from the lower right-hand corner of 'Lower Lincoln's Inn Fields' to Fleet Street, but today we must make our way down Serle Street and turn left to Carey Street (also as in Walk 1), then right into Chancery Lane, and zig-zag briefly across Fleet Street before continuing south down Middle Temple Lane to Middle Temple Hall. And the reason for doing so is not only to admire the Hall itself – which is a Tudor survivor dating from about 1562–1573, with a double hammer-beam roof to rival that of Westminster Hall, and a notable oak screen and Elizabethan high table – but because this was where the first recorded public performance of *Twelfth Night* took place on 2 February 1602. You will have to ask the staff on the door if they will let you look inside, but they are proud of it themselves and will always agree to do so if they can. (There is also the option of booking an official tour round the site, but you will need to gather a group of ten to do so.) Shakespeare himself was almost certainly one of the actors for this first performance, bringing his company over from the Globe in Southwark. Indeed, this is our last stop on the north side of the Thames before we head to Southwark ourselves via the Victoria Embankment and Blackfriars Bridge. But before doing so, 'range about' the Middle Temple, as Pepys did himself on the afternoon of 25 November 1660. There is still plenty to enjoy here – Temple Church, with its nine effigies of crusader knights (this round church was consecrated for the Knights Templar by a different but actual Heraclius, the Patriarch of Jerusalem, in 1185) and rectangular chancel dating from 1240; and the seventeenth-century Pump Court. All very different to the noise of Blackfriars Bridge, the bracing open air and bustle of the river, and then the rough and tumble of Southwark itself. Walk over the bridge now.

What is it about the left banks of cities such as London or Paris that they become the haunt of the bohemian, the illicit, the sometimes downright dangerous, and the setting for adventures you might hesitate to recount, once safely back at home? Southwark in Pepys's day had all the wicked pleasures you could ask for. Much of the land here belonged to the Bishops of Winchester and, far from suppressing the bawdy goings-on, they made a great deal of money out of them: they licensed the brothels or 'stews' (of which there were dozens – the sex workers within them were known as 'Winchester Geese') and, if things got too out of hand, they threw the wrongdoers into their very own prison, the Clink. At nine o'clock every night, the drawbridge that joined Southwark to London Bridge was raised, and after that the night's entertainment really got going. There were the theatres, the Globe being but one; after these closed at six o'clock there was bull- and bear-baiting, cockfighting, prizefighting, gaming houses, the brothels (of course), street performances of all sorts (Pepys saw the tight-rope walker Jacob Hall here in 1668) and any number of taverns in which to sleep it all off. Yet today there is also the sublimely peaceful Southwark Cathedral and the delectable Borough Market, London's open-air delicatessen, where you will find the best street food the capital has to offer, and down on Borough High Street itself, an echo of Geoffrey Chaucer and his Canterbury pilgrims setting off from the Tabard Inn. We will come to them all.

First stop after leaving Blackfriars Bridge: pick up the Thames Path, and follow the curvature of the rail station façade to bear right onto Hopton Street and right onto Holland Street. Holland Street is named after one Bess Holland, who in the first three decades of the seventeenth century ran London's biggest, smartest, most luxurious and exclusive brothel, Holland's Leaguer, at a spot which is now under Blackfriars Station but which can be identified on those early perspective maps of the period by the fact that it was moated. An old manor house originally, Holland's Leaguer was reputed to have had James I and the Duke of Buckingham among its patrons, and it was famous enough to inspire in its honour a ballad as well as a stage play by one Shackerley Marmion, first performed at the Salisbury Court playhouse (the one near to Pepys's birthplace) in 1631. Charles I closed down Holland's Leaguer, not without difficulty, in January 1632. Amusingly, the street now named in its honour is the very one where the inhabitants of the multi-million-pound apartments in NEO Bankside have objected so strenuously to the fact that visitors to the Tate could look into their bedrooms – something that would have worried the inhabitants of Holland's Leaguer not at all.

Make your way back to the Thames Path and the river, go past the Tate Modern, and there on your right is a tiny little alleyway – Cardinal Cap Alley – between a Queen Anne-ish looking low brick house and a stucco-faced one, very tall and thin as if it were holding its breath, which dates in fact from 1650. This was where, according to Stow, a run of common-or-garden brothels began: the Castle upon the Hoop, the Antelope, the Swan, the Bullhead, the Crane, the Elephant, the Lion, the Heart, to name but a few, all with their signs painted on the walls beside their doors. (If you look across the river at this point, you will see the modern Samuel Pepys pub, behind which is Stew Lane. Guess what went on there, as well!) The brothels along this part of the south bank of the river ran until one reached the Anchor public house – look back when we get there later and imagine what these streets would have been like in Pepys's time. We have the names of two further famous 'bawds' from this period: one was Elizabeth Cresswell, who advertised herself as offering 'Beauties of all Complexions, from the cole-black clyng-fast to the golden lock'd insatiate, from the sleepy ey'd Slug to the lewd Fricatrix', and who operated brothels in Little Britain and Lincoln's

Inn Fields, and died around 1698; the other was Damaris Page, who Pepys described in 1668 as 'the Most Famous Bawd in the Towne'. Popular feeling sometimes overflowed against London's brothels, and one such moment was in March 1668. On the 25th of that month Pepys writes:

> The Duke of York and all with him this morning were full of the talk of the 'prentices, who are not yet [put] down, though the guards and militia of the town have been in armes all this night, and the night before; and the 'prentices have made fools of them, sometimes by running from them and flinging stones at them. Some blood hath been spilt, but a great many houses pulled down; and, among others, the Duke of York was mighty merry at that of Damaris Page's, the great bawd of the seamen...

In response, the bawds created a satirical letter, 'The Poor Whores' Petition', which, to her fury, was addressed to the king's mistress, Barbara Villiers, as a 'sister'.

Next door to Cardinal Cap Alley is the reconstructed Globe. Pepys saw a number of Shakespearean productions in his theatre-going (although not necessarily on the south bank). *The Tempest*, which he saw on 7 November 1667, again with Sir William Penn, struck him as

> the most innocent play that ever I saw; and a curious piece of musique in an echo of half sentences, the echo repeating the former half, while the man goes on to the latter; which is mighty pretty. The play [has] no great wit, but yet good, above ordinary plays.

He was, however, a big fan of *Macbeth*, seeing two productions in quick order over Christmas 1666:

> though I saw it lately, yet appears a most excellent play in all respects, but especially in divertisement, though it be a deep tragedy; which is a strange perfection in a tragedy, it being most proper here, and suitable.

Carry on along the Thames Path, and on the corner of a building on your right, you'll see the 'Ferryman's Seat' – really just an odd little lump of stone, like a hearthstone, but set at seat-level in an alcove. These used to line the riverbank, providing a more or less sheltered place for a Thames waterman to rest as he waited for his next customers to ferry up or down the river. Thames watermen were not only notoriously foul-mouthed but mightily muscled as well, with all that rowing. Just south of the Thames Path here (you will have to turn back on yourself and go via New Globe Walk, then east on Park Street) is the site of the Bear Gardens. Pepys was here on 14 September 1666 and 'saw some good sport of the bull's tossing of the dogs – one into the very boxes. But it is a very rude and nasty pleasure'. He was here again to see a prize fight between a butcher and a waterman on 27 May 1667, where what sounds like a monumental brawl broke out:

> The former had the better all along, till by and by the latter dropped his sword out of his hand, and the butcher, whether not seeing his sword dropped I know not, but did give him a cut over the wrist, so as he was disabled to fight any longer. But, Lord! to see how in a minute the whole stage was full of watermen to revenge the foul play, and the butchers to defend their fellow, though most blamed him; and there they all fell

to it to knocking down and cutting many on each side. It was pleasant to see, but that I stood in the pit, and feared that in the tumult I might get some hurt.

Head to the end of Park Street and then back to the river, and carry on eastwards along Bankside until you come to the Anchor. Although it's always crowded, I am a big fan of the Anchor. Its interior has the feel of having been nailed together from any number of bits of timber and panelling and little runs of staircases salvaged from Tudor galleons. And it was here that Pepys came himself, it's thought, on the fateful night of the Great Fire to watch its progress:

> ... and there staid till it was dark almost, and saw the Fire grow... it made me weep to see it. The churches, houses and all on fire, and flaming at once; and a horrid noise the flames made, and the cracking of houses at their ruins.

Next along in Southwark's charms is the Clink Prison Museum, a little way further down the path. This is much more of a tourist attraction than a historic site these days, the original having been burned down during the anti-Catholic Gordon Riots in 1780, but right next door you'll find all that's left of the once-gorgeous Winchester Palace, seat of the Bishops of Winchester, built with all their ill-gotten gains, and with the stonework for a particularly lovely rose window. Just along from here, in St Mary Overie Dock, you'll find a reconstruction of Sir Francis Drake's *Golden Hinde*, looking to us almost too small to trust oneself to it on the Thames, let alone to circumnavigate the globe. Somehow a crew of eighty squeezed themselves into the original, of which this is an exact copy, and between 1577 and 1580 did indeed sail round the world.

Ahead of you now you'll see London Bridge. Be aware, the bridge has moved upstream since Pepys's day. Where the old bridge originally made landfall on this side of the river – now just the other side of London Bridge – was the Beare tavern, and a sad tale, which Pepys learned from his waterman as he travelled home on the night of 24 February 1667:

> This night going through bridge by water, my waterman told me how the mistress of the Beare tavern, at the bridge-foot, did lately fling herself into the Thames, and drowned herself; which did trouble me the more, when they tell me it was she that did live at the White Horse tavern in Lumbard Streete, which was [the] most beautiful woman, as most I have seen. It seems she hath had long melancholy upon her, and hath endeavoured to make away with herself often.

Spare a thought for her as you come up to Southwark Cathedral, although the cathedral is such a perfect oasis of calm it is hard to feel any emotion inside it but wonder. Shakespeare worshipped here, the early English poet John Gower is buried here, and it has a chapel to local boy John Harvard, founder of Harvard University. And all around it is Borough Market where, having restored your spirit in the Cathedral, you can restore your body from any of the many stalls selling every kind of food imaginable.

Thus restored, walk south down Borough High Street. On your left you will come to the George Inn, the only galleried coaching inn left in London. The present building dates from 1677 but there has been an inn on this site since around 1542. Not far from here stood its twin, the Tabard, from which Chaucer's pilgrims set off on their journey to Canterbury (Talbot Yard, next door to the George, marks its site), and the one remaining double-height galleried side of the George's courtyard, or something like it, is what you might imagine them as having carried in their heads when they set off, and still gives a good idea of the scale of such inns, and their animation and conviviality, not to mention commercial confidence. Dickens was here too, and he mentions it in *Little Dorrit*. But tear yourself away and carry on down the High Street until you reach Union Street on the right. Walk one block along this, turn off right, and a little way down you will see a gated garden, the railings draped with a vivid curtain of jewellery, hung about with plastic flowers and even the odd lipstick or eyeliner. This is Crossbones Garden, the last resting place of thousands of Southwark women who made their living in its brothels. Says Stow:

> ... these single woman were forbidden the rites of the church, so long as they continued that sinful life, and were excluded from Christian burial, if they were not reconciled before their death. And therefore there was a plot of ground called the Single Women's churchyard, appointed for them far from the parish church.

And here they lie in graves that date back, some of them, to the Middle Ages, many of them with their children too – unborn, still-born, or victims of childhood diseases that barely exist these days. Many of their mothers died heartbreakingly young as well, ravaged by tuberculosis or worse. The graveyard closed only in 1853, 'completely overcharged with dead', as it was described at the time, and since then the site has been threatened numerous times with redevelopment and being built over. The local community, however, has taken these women to its heart and created this garden to preserve the old graveyard and the remains of those who lie within it, and decorated the ugly chain-link fence with jewellery for the women and even toys for the children, as if to atone for their suffering in the past.

It was not only the sex workers who ended their days here. Come back to the High Street and carry on walking until you reach Little Dorrit Park. Opposite is Angel Place. Walk down Angel Place, past the John Harvard Library, until you reach a long run of brownish brick wall. As the plaque here states, this marks what was the boundary of London's debtor's prison, the Marshalsea (the library occupies its actual site), where Little Dorrit's father is incarcerated in Dickens's novel of 1855 and where in real life the infamous brothel keeper Damaris Page was incarcerated, became sick, and died on 9 October 1669. If, as you may feel moved to do, you end this walk in the church of St George the Martyr next door, you will be where she was buried, although we have no record of where. You might, while you are there, spare a thought not only for Damaris but for the generations of unknown women who worked for her and for others like her. Borough Tube station is just on the other side of the road, ready to take you back to twenty-first-century London. A night out with Mr Pepys might in some ways have been riotously good fun, but for all the perils our modern world must battle through, especially at the time of writing, it's worth remembering that one stands a far better chance of returning safely home from such a ramble today.

Along the River to Greenwich

THIS IS A WALK into a different side of Pepys's professional life: the hands-on naval administrator. It takes us away from the court and its gossip and intrigues, and into the world of the victualling yards, the rope works, and the docks. We'll set out from Seething Lane, as Pepys did many a time, walk over Tower Bridge to Southwark, and from there go all the way down to Greenwich. Assume at least twelve kilometres or seven-and-a-half miles and most of the day for this walk – longer on both counts if you want to end it with a trip to Greenwich's Royal Observatory.

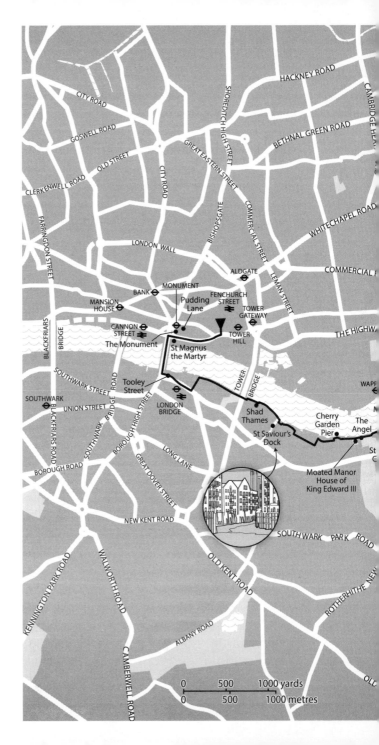

HACKNEY ROAD

CAMBRIDGE HEA

CITY ROAD

GOSWELL ROAD

BETHNAL GREEN ROAD

OLD STREET

CLERKENWELL ROAD

GREAT EASTERN STREET

SHOREDITCH HIGH STREET

CITY ROAD

WHITECHAPEL ROAD

FARRINGDON STREET

LONDON WALL

BISHOPSGATE

COMMERCIAL STREET

ALDGATE

COMMERCIAL F

MONUMENT

BANK

FENCHURCH
STREET

LEMAN STREET

MANSION
HOUSE

Pudding
Lane

TOWER
GATEWAY

CANNON
STREET

THE HIGHW

BLACKFRIARS
BRIDGE

The Monument

TOWER
HILL

St Magnus
the Martyr

TOWER BRIDGE

SOUTHWARK STREET

Tooley
Street

WAPF

SOUTHWARK BRIDGE ROAD

SOUTHWARK

UNION STREET

LONDON
BRIDGE

Shad
Thames

Cherry
Garden
Pier

The
Angel

BLACKFRIARS ROAD

BOROUGH HIGH STREET

St Saviour's
Dock

St
C

LONG LANE

BOROUGH ROAD

GREAT DOVER STREET

Moated Manor
House of
King Edward III

NEW KENT ROAD

SOUTHWARK PARK ROAD

KENNINGTON PARK ROAD

WALWORTH ROAD

OLD KENT ROAD

ROTHERHITHE NEW

ALBANY ROAD

OLD

CAMBERWELL ROAD

| 0 | 500 | 1000 yards |
| 0 | 500 | 1000 metres |

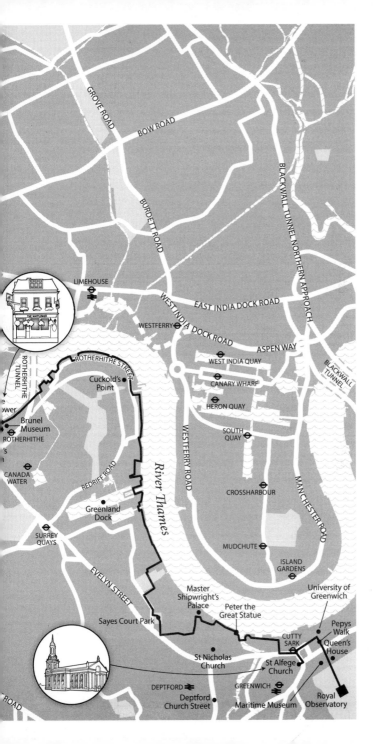

GROVE ROAD

BOW ROAD

BURDETT ROAD

BLACKWALL TUNNEL NORTHERN APPROACH

LIMEHOUSE

THE MAYFLOWER

EAST INDIA DOCK ROAD

WEST INDIA DOCK ROAD

WESTFERRY

ASPEN WAY

WEST INDIA QUAY

BLACKWALL TUNNEL

ROTHERHITHE TUNNEL

ROTHERHITHE STREET

Cuckold's Point

CANARY WHARF

HERON QUAY

Brunel Museum

ROTHERHITHE

WESTFERRY ROAD

SOUTH QUAY

CANADA WATER

REDRIFF ROAD

River Thames

CROSSHARBOUR

MANCHESTER ROAD

Greenland Dock

SURREY QUAYS

MUDCHUTE

ISLAND GARDENS

EVELYN STREET

Master Shipwright's Palace

University of Greenwich

Peter the Great Statue

Sayes Court Park

Pepys Walk

CUTTY SARK

Queen's House

St Nicholas Church

St Alfege Church

DEPTFORD

GREENWICH

Deptford Church Street

Maritime Museum

Royal Observatory

ROAD

We'll start at St Olave's, 'our own church' as Pepys described it, in Seething Lane. John Stow in 1598 records no fewer than four churches in London named St Olave's, all in honour of King Olaf II, the patron saint of Norway, who fought alongside the Anglo-Saxon King Æthelred 'the Unready' against the Danes at the Battle of London Bridge in 1014. Olaf is meant to have destroyed the existing bridge and thus prevented the Viking forces in Southwark from reinforcing their fellows on the north bank of the river, and this (possibly, perhaps) inspired the nursery rhyme 'London Bridge is Falling Down'. London has not only many layers but a long, long memory too, and all the way through this walk we will encounter reminders of her maritime friends and foes.

Head down Seething Lane to Byward Street and Lower Thames Street, which in Pepys's time marked the rough edge of the north bank of the river, and walk towards London Bridge. I so wish London still had its old bridge. Imagine if this extraordinary, gravity-defying, Gormenghast-esque gateau, this centuries-long accretion of stone and timber, had survived. If you detour here slightly off Lower Thames Street, stand in front of the Monument to the Great Fire, and look beyond St Magnus the Martyr to the south bank, you will be in line with the bridge's original position (a plaque in the churchyard records how it was part of the approach to the bridge). St Magnus's church is another link to the north, being named for St Magnus Earl of Orkney and, when you have time, it is worth another detour to get to know it properly, not least because it contains a gorgeous model of London Bridge at the time of Henry V, who is himself one of the 900 tiny figures making their way across it. The present church is one of Wren's; the original, which dated back to 1128, was an early victim of the Great Fire, having narrowly survived a more local conflagration in February 1633 when a careless maidservant (it's always some poor maidservant who gets the blame) left a pan of hot ashes under a wooden stepladder. Forty-two houses were consumed until this particular fire reached 'a vacancy'. The householders couldn't even use water from the river to fight the flames: this being February and in the epoch of Europe's Little Ice Age, the Thames, as Stow records, 'was almost frozen over'.

But, of course, the fire everyone thinks of when they think of Samuel Pepys is the Great Fire of London in 1666. This began in the middle of the night on Sunday 2 September in the oven of Thomas Farriner, a baker, in Pudding Lane. The summer of 1666 had been extremely hot and dry, there was a strong east wind, and Londoners' shops and houses – made of timber, wattle and daub (basically, straw and clay) and roofed with thatch – went up like the tinder they were. This was essentially therefore a forest fire, with tens of thousands of people fleeing from it with everything they could carry. The emphasis on escape, rather than on fighting the flames, let it spread beyond control, and it took hours before the authorities realised what they were dealing with; on seeing flames from a distance, the Lord Mayor, Thomas Bloodworth, reputedly first reacted with: 'A woman could piss it out.' Pepys, viewing the same from the church tower of All Hallows-by-the-Tower (another survivor), came to a different conclusion: 'An infinite great fire on this and the other side the end of the bridge', and set off by boat to Whitehall without delay, carrying the news to the king and to James, Duke of York, in person: the whole of the City was in peril.

Pepys speaks of how, by this point, 'with one's face in the wind, you were almost burned with a shower of firedrops', of the Fire having 'a most horrid malicious bloody flame, not like the fine flame of an ordinary fire'. Of course not; it was now being fed by warehouse after warehouse of pitch, hemp, resin and flax, cellars full of coal and barrels of spirits, and the riverside shacks of London's poorest inhabitants. Pepys, in the Anchor on Bankside (see Walk 3), saw it as 'only one entire arch of fire from this to the other side [of] the bridge, and in a bow up the hill for an arch of above a mile long'.

By Monday, Samuel and Elizabeth and their entire household were resigning themselves to losing everything they could not carry away or bury, and still the Fire raged on, from one district, one street, to the next. By Tuesday, it looked as if the flames might leap the firebreak on London Bridge and consume Southwark – and even get to Whitehall. 'Walking into the garden', he records, on Tuesday night,

> and saw how horridly the sky looks, all on a fire in the night, was enough to put us out of our wits; and, indeed, it was extremely dreadful, for it looks just as if it was at us; and the whole heaven on fire.

Finally, on Wednesday, the blowing-up and tearing down of houses began to have some effect. And the wind dropped, and it rained. Pepys, thinking strategically as ever, got up high into the steeple of All Hallows again:

> and there saw the saddest sight of desolation that I ever saw; every where great fires, oyle-cellars, and brimstone, and other things burning. I became afeard to stay there long, and therefore down again as fast as I could, the fire being spread as far as I could see it...

From Sunday to Wednesday, he records, 'felt like a week or more.'

For all its sixty-two-metre height, the Monument to the Fire, put up between 1671 and 1677, hardly seems enough of an acknowledgement of what Pepys and his fellow Londoners went through on those four days – and indeed for months to come. In total, the Fire took 13,200 houses, 87 churches, and 52 livery halls, and some three-quarters of the City. The traditional view that only a handful of people perished in the flames has been re-examined too: the Fire reached temperatures of 1,250°C, the same as that of a crematorium. Of anyone caught in it, there would literally have been nothing left; their ashes would have been mixed with those of the houses, the churches, Old St Paul's, the Royal Exchange, and every other building that had stood in the Fire's path. Thank heaven for the river. Thank heaven for that firebreak on the bridge.

London Bridge linked London's two halves as the *corpus callosum* does the two halves of the human brain. Whoever controlled it controlled London, as Æthelred and Olaf understood full well. And it is mentioned on almost every page of the Diary. First of all, it had two of Pepys's favourite watering holes at either end of it – the Hoops, near St Magnus, and the Beare at the Bridge Foot on its southern end – and it was part of his almost daily ritual to pick up a boat at the bridge to go down to Greenwich or up to Westminster, if the tide was cooperative. (In the past, Londoners must have carried a perpetual tide table in their heads much as today we keep a mental tally of which Underground lines are running and which not.) When the war with the Dutch oozed up the Thames estuary, had the Dutch at any point seized London Bridge they might well have seized the City too – and at those times it was understood that the bridge was to be defended at all costs. June 1667, after the shocking raid on the Medway by the Dutch, was one of those worrying times. On the 13th of that month, Pepys records that:

The King and Duke of York have been below [i.e. on the river
below London Bridge] since four o'clock in the morning, to
command the sinking of ships at Barking-Creeke, and other
places, to stop [the Dutch] coming up higher: which put me
into such a fear, that I presently resolved of my father's and
wife's going into the country; and, at two hours' warning, they
did go by the coach this day, with about 1300*l*. in gold in their
night-bag.

Barking Creek is about sixteen kilometres or ten miles downriver –
nothing, if you're facing an invasion.

Almost as alarming was Pepys's experience of the bridge on
26 October 1664. Returning from Woolwich in the dark, he had
already given a lift to a woman on her way to London when his coach
hit a 'stop' in Southwark. Tired of waiting for the stop to clear, Sam
got down, saw the coach of a naval colleague, Sir William Batten,
and in this seventeenth-century traffic jam joined Sir William at the
Beare. When they emerged, Sam's coach had driven off.

... so I fair to go through the darke and dirt over the bridge,
and my leg fell in a hole broke on the bridge, but, the constable
standing there to keep people from it, I was catched up, otherwise
I had broke my leg; for which mercy the Lord be praised!

A broken leg in 1664 might well have meant amputation – or worse.
Cross the Thames yourself by London Bridge, without incident,
please, and turn east onto Tooley Street – which, in one of those
historic slippages of pronunciation, also commemorates St Olave,
although quite how one gets from him to 'Tooley' boggles the mind.
As soon as you can, turn towards the river again, perhaps up the

pleasingly named Battle Bridge Lane, and follow the Thames Path along the river to the foot of Tower Bridge. You are now in Shad Thames.

Shad Thames is a splendid example of how the tides of history in a city wash in and out (especially here), each one adding another layer of use and character and local population. Those gantries running overhead date back to the district's commercial heyday in the nineteenth century, as ship after ship unloaded here into warehouse after warehouse. But back in Pepys's day, Faithorne and Newcourt's map shows little more than a single street (now Bermondsey Wall West) along the river, lined on both sides with houses, many of which on the landward side had large gardens behind them and open country beyond that, commemorated here in names such as Horselydown (i.e. horse-lie-down) Lane.

Walk with the bars and restaurants and luxury apartments on your right and the river on the left. Go past the blue plaque to the filmmaker Derek Jarman, who lived and worked here before it was all quite so tidied up, and you will see ahead of you an unassuming inlet (the last remaining trickle of the River Neckinger) with a footbridge. This, known to John Stow as 'Savary Dock', is now St Saviour's Dock, and here again we cross paths with Charles Dickens and a trio of small boys because this, in *Oliver Twist*, was the site of the death of Bill Sikes. In actual nineteenth-century London, this was 'Jacob's Island', one of London's most appalling slums or so-called 'rookeries', and a notorious court to 'King Cholera'. Dickens, with that passion of his for London at its seamiest, described it thus:

Crazy wooden galleries common to the backs of half a
dozen houses, with holes from which to look upon the slime
beneath; windows, broken and patched... In Jacob's Island, the

warehouses are roofless and empty; the walls are crumbling down; the windows are windows no more; the doors are falling into the streets... Thirty or forty years ago... it was a thriving place; but now it is a desolate island indeed. The houses have no owners; they are broken open, and entered upon by those who have the courage; and there they live, and there they die.

If you happen to cross that footbridge at low tide, with the grey-green Thames mud waiting beneath you, you can still, with a frisson, get some idea of how it must have looked in Dickens's day. Jacob's Island is still remembered in Jacob Street, to the south. After Oliver, the second small boy is Pepys himself who, in that curious incident from his childhood, recalled being sent to St Saviour's Dock to glean news of his father, who was away on his mysterious mission to Holland. And now you are on Bermondsey Wall West where the third little boy greets you in Banksy's *Boy Fishing*, much faded at time of writing from its original condition – a little ghost of itself, perhaps.

Turn right via George Row to find Chambers Street, and then left down Loftie Street to get onto Bermondsey Wall East. It is extraordinary how the crowds fall away once you get past Shad Thames, and now you are once again walking in Pepys's footsteps, past a picturesque settling of houseboats (or whatever the collective noun for them may be). Give yourself a moment here to try to imagine the Thames as it was in Pepys's day. To your left, imagine the shoreline with muddy inlets and wide bands of shingle or of sand, with seagulls everywhere, just as today, and the odd heron and swan as well. Were there seals too, one wonders? Did whales ever wander upstream, as they sometimes do today? Certainly the Thames was full of fish, with many a waterside inn serving little else – such as the 'jole' of salmon purchased by Pepys for his dinner party in Walk 3. To your right, there would have been orchards, including cherry orchards, water meadows with windmills and farmhouses, and the odd larger tavern for those visitors enjoying a day in the countryside. One such was Jamaica House, which would have stood behind you, back from the river's edge, and which survived into the 1880s. Engravings show a building of two storeys with that unmistakable, boxy seventeenth-century shape and a very pretty garden behind, to be enjoyed from a first-storey veranda running the length of the building at the back – the perfect place to enjoy the view. Pepys went there for the first time in April 1667 accompanied by his wife and Mary Mercer, who had been Elizabeth's companion from 1664 to 1666, as well as Mary's mother, who was a neighbour back at Crutched Friars (and Will Hewer's landlady), and two of his maids. While there, 'the girls did run for wagers over the bowling-green'. It seems to have been an afternoon of rare accord among the women in Sam's household. Jamaica House is remembered today in Jamaica Road, also known as the A200, which runs through Bermondsey, past Surrey Quays, and on into Greenwich. Our route will be rather more scenic and far quieter.

On the far side of the river you'd have been looking over at Wapping – significantly more built up than here in Bermondsey, but with the same maritime profile of warehouses, quays, and cranes. On both sides of the river, stone steps or wooden piers would lead down into the water as regularly as bus stops along a street today, and the Thames itself, London's greatest highway for centuries, would be full of ships and boats of every shape and size – three-masters, carracks, row-boats, ferries, barges, splendid galleons in full sail, and little fishing smacks. The nineteenth-century artist James McNeill Whistler painted his magnificent oil *Wapping: The Thames* from the Angel public house (which we will come to shortly) in the 1860s, showing a river so thronged with craft you can barely see across to Wapping on its other side, and you have to imagine it as being very much like that in Pepys's day as well. The other addition you would have to make to the scene would of course be a smudge of bronchial-brown coal smoke, lying pretty much permanently in the London sky above the north bank of the river.

But before the Angel is Cherry Garden Pier and another direct link to Sam. He was here on the evening of 13 June 1664 buying cherries, which he carried home to Elizabeth, with the happy result that they made love 'which from my not being thoroughly well, nor she, we have not done above once these two or three weeks'. Pepys liked cherries – all Londoners did, with the street vendor's cry of 'Cherry ripe!' inspiring the poets Thomas Campion and Robert Herrick. A little further on and old Rotherhithe's delightful and historical character begins to disclose itself. First, on your right, a grassy square holding the remains of some ancient and very heavy-duty masonry. This is all that is left of the walls of a moated manor house used by King Edward III – moated because in its day it stood proud of the shoreline, which by Pepys's time had already silted and filled in around it, while the walls of the royal residence itself had become melded into those of a local pottery, the sort of architectural transubstantiation at which London excels.

Then, to your left, you will find an intriguing little group of statues – an elderly man, a woman in Edwardian dress, a little girl, and a cat. This is *Dr Salter's Daydream*. Dr Salter was a Quaker physician who devoted himself to the care of the people of Bermondsey, becoming the Labour MP for Bermondsey West in 1922. His wife, Ada, was to become the first woman mayor of a London borough; but their daughter, Joyce, the little girl, died of scarlet fever at the age of eight. The 'daydream' is of course of the family reunited, complete with the family pet.

And so we come to the Angel, a tavern which (we are told) Pepys knew well, although the present building dates from the 1830s. The wooden balcony seen in Whistler's painting is still there, overhanging the Thames, and there is a trapdoor in the building's floor leading straight down into the river and much appreciated, one imagines, by the smugglers who are supposed to have made this a favourite haunt. Rather less appealingly, Pepys's contemporary, the notorious Judge Jeffreys – the 'Hanging Judge', who is going to haunt these last two walks like the bogeyman he was – is supposed to have used the Angel to view the last agonies of the many he had sentenced to death, hanging over the river in Wapping's Execution Dock – in which case, along with a pair of the heaviest eyebrows in British legal history, the judge must have had quite exceptional eyesight. But there is a little mystery here. There was certainly a tavern on this site for centuries, and Pepys must have walked past it many a time, but although there are dozens of mentions of Rotherhithe – or Redriffe, as it was known then – in the Diary, and at least two taverns named 'The Angell', neither of them was here.

Keep strolling along the Thames path until you get to Rotherhithe Street. At almost two-and-a-half kilometres, this is the longest street in London and will carry you into Rotherhithe proper. Take a short detour here, turning right down St Marychurch Street. The streets here are cobbled, the noise of London far away, and you might almost expect to see eighteenth-century schoolchildren file sedately from the door of the charming 'free school' you will pass on your left – another building that seems far too small for its historical purpose, like St Olave's. The statues of two of its putative pupils stand over the door, an eighteenth-century boy and girl in period dress, and there is more historical costume in the window above you of the prop-and-costume store, looking down benignly onto the street like ghostly manifestations of Rotherhithe's one-time inhabitants. Now turn around and walk back up St Marychurch Street towards Rotherhithe Street. On your left you will see St Mary's Church and, along the street beyond it, the Mayflower pub. There has been a tavern here since 1550, and it and the church have a significant historical connection: Captain Christopher Jones, master of the *Mayflower*, moored his ship here before sailing with the Pilgrim Fathers to the New World in 1620. Jones must have liked Rotherhithe; he moved his family here from Essex in 1611 and, after all his adventures, was buried somewhere in St Mary's Churchyard in 1622. It's rather humbling that no one thought him of enough importance at the time to record exactly where. The little church itself is a survivor of more or less continual flooding, with its parishioners, in 1710, left to shore it up and pretty much rebuild it themselves. They did an excellent job.

St Mary's is well worth investigating inside. A plaque on the wall records another lost burial, of one Prince Lee Boo of Palau in the Western Pacific, who arrived in London in 1784 with Captain Henry Wilson of the *Antelope*. The *Antelope* had been wrecked off Palau in 1783 when Wilson's crew were saved by Lee Boo's father, Ibedul, the local ruler. The adventurous Lee Boo, joining Wilson on an information-gathering trip for his father, became the toast of London and lived with the Wilsons in Rotherhithe for just six months before he contracted smallpox, poor lad. Just as poignant: J. M. W. Turner painted *The Fighting Temeraire* from studies made while HMS *Temeraire* was in the breaker's yard in Rotherhithe. He had spotted this one-time heroine of the Battle of Trafalgar being ignominiously tugged upriver while he was himself boating off the Greenwich marshes. Turner's masterpiece, with the *Temeraire* looking as if she has already slipped into some silvery, otherworldly, and more honourable realm, is in the National Gallery, but some of the ship's timbers are here in the church, refashioned into a communion table and bishops' chairs.

In honour of Christopher Jones's exceptional New World voyage, the Mayflower is the only pub in the UK that can sell you US postage stamps. If by now you should find yourself 'pretty weary and all of a sweat', as Samuel Pepys did walking through Rotherhithe in September 1662, I suggest you duck into the Mayflower to refresh yourself.

It's yet further tribute to Rotherhithe's seafaring connections that Jonathan Swift used it as the birthplace of his traveller Lemuel Gulliver in *Gulliver's Travels* (1726). Rotherhithe also boasts the Brunel Museum, dedicated to the nineteenth-century iron-man and engineer Isambard Kingdom Brunel, who built the SS *Great Eastern*, the largest ship in the world at the time of her launch in 1858. And it is home to the Norwegian Church and Seamen's Mission in London, a stone's throw away in St Olav's Square. (Until 2012 there was a Swedish Seamen's Church here too, and there is still a Finnish Seamen's Mission.) But Christopher Jones, and his voyage, is by far the most noteworthy.

If your ears now pick up a low hum, never fear – this is the Rotherhithe Tunnel, and another part of Rotherhithe's history. Opened in 1908, it links the south bank of the river with Limehouse. Leave it behind you, and carry on along Rotherhithe Street, crossing the inlet to Surrey Water (not to be confused with Surrey Quays) via the thrilling red-painted 'bascule' or see-saw bridge. Sadly this no longer see-saws, but it's a marvellous-looking piece of engineering even so. Go left whenever you please after the bridge and pick up the Thames Path again, beside the river, where you will find yourself in a very different environment altogether, of gated communities and neo-Georgian architecture, vanilla in both conception and colour. Yes, I know it has been a little while since we heard anything from Sam, but we will meet up with him again very soon. In the meantime, even if the architecture immediately around you is depressingly samey, take a moment to enjoy the wonderful views of the river and the opposite shore. This is the part of the walk where any remaining cobwebs will be well and truly blown away, and where you can begin to appreciate just what a huge river the Thames truly is – far larger than the Seine, for example – and quite how horribly easy it would have been for an unwary captain, having brought his ship perfectly safely up from Bordeaux or over from Holland, to come tragically unstuck as he tried to navigate the twisting currents and contrariwise gusting winds of the Thames Valley, especially where the river makes that unmistakable big swinging curve around the Isle of Dogs. The job of Thames pilot, for the men who could read the river's moods, was not only lucrative but prestigious. Pepys knew at least one such by name: Augustine Punnet. He also had sympathy for the equally treacherous professional waters these men had to navigate. In October 1666, he records a conversation with Colonel Thomas Middleton, Navy Commissioner of Portsmouth:

> the pilots do say, that they dare not do nor go but as the
> Captains will have them; and if they offer to do otherwise,
> the Captains swear they will run them through.

And this is where we re-join Samuel Pepys, and share again his experience of the river in his own words. Walking through Rotherhithe on 24 January 1666 with Lord Brouncker, Pepys records that the wind was so 'furious' that they did not dare take a boat home, and even walking 'so strong [was] the wind, that in the fields we many times could not carry our bodies against it, but were driven backwards'. It's a phenomenon familiar to those of us who live along the river, even today. Arriving at London Bridge, Pepys reports,

> the greatest sight of all was, among other parcels of ships driven here and there in clusters together, one was quite overset and lay with her masts all along in the water, and keel above water.

The Thames Path here winds in and out, and annoyingly in some places it is blocked by new housing developments, in which case you will have to cut inland, though only for a hundred metres or so. When Pepys walked along the river, all buildings on this side stopped at Surrey Water, while on the north shore there would have been nothing more after Limehouse Basin.

The path will eventually take you right around the top of Rotherhithe, past the curiously named Cuckold's Point. This spot was well known in Pepys's day and features in the 1630 *Works* of John Taylor, the 'Water Poet'. It is also mentioned by the playwright William Congreve and referenced (very rudely) by Hogarth's *Idle 'Prentice* of 1747. There's a legend of a lumpish miller with a pretty wife, all to explain the tradition of setting up a pole festooned with horns here at the water's edge – which sounds positively Celtic to me. It gave Londoners an excuse for the 'Horn Fair', another local Bacchanalia that the po-faced Victorians suppressed, but which in recent years has had a small, rather more family-friendly, revival.

And here at Cuckold's Point we encounter Pepys again. He was carried past this very place in the *Charles*, a royal yacht, on another blustery day: 20 February 1663. It seems to have been his first trip in a small sailboat:

I could have been sick if I would in going, the wind being very
fresh, but very pleasant it was, and the first time I have sailed in
any one of them. It carried us to Cuckold's Point, and so by oars
to the Temple.

Clearly those who knew the river knew where best one went by sail
and where best by rowing.

You're now coming down the eastern edge of Rotherhithe and
facing a cityscape that to Pepys would have been simply unbeliev-
able – that of the Isle of Dogs.

In Pepys's time, the Isle of Dogs was almost unpopulated, noted
only for its value as grazing land for fattening cattle on their way
to Smithfield Market; it was far from the mini-Manhattan it has
become today. The old river wall holding back the waters from that
part of the Isle of Dogs now opposite you had been broken by a
storm in 1488, creating a marsh known as 'the Breach', and so little
regarded was the area that the Breach is still there in John Rocque's
map of 1746. Behind it was a body of standing water known as
'Poplar Gut'. In essence, this meant that the island was pretty much
cut off from the whole of the rest of London at every high tide or
even after heavy rain. Pepys himself was stranded here in 1665, the
plague year, with Sir George and Lady Carteret, all in their finest,
while trying to get to a wedding (because, of course, these mishaps
never happen when one is simply in a hurry to get to the shops).

Up, and very betimes by six o'clock at Deptford, and there find
Sir G. Carteret, and my Lady ready to go: I being in my new
coloured silk suit, and coat trimmed with gold buttons and
gold broad lace round my hands, very rich and fine. By water
to the Ferry, where, when we come, no coach there; and tide

of ebb so far spent as the horse-boat could not get off on the other side the river to bring away the coach. So we were fain to stay there in the unlucky Isle of Doggs, in a chill place, the morning cool, and wind fresh, above two if not three hours to our great discontent.

Almost the only settled area of the Isle of Dogs was in its north-east corner, where a shingle spit gave a firm enough foundation for a shipyard, contemporary with Pepys and belonging to the East India Company. Otherwise, the entire island up to the village of Poplar was field and marsh and grazing cattle. What would Pepys make of it now?

This is one of the parts of the walk where you have to come off the Thames Path, to walk round the DoubleTree Hilton Hotel. The (now landlocked) dock here is the Nelson Dock. Its connection to Nelson is as tangential as is Cuckold's Point to any particular cuckold, but the connection to Pepys is real enough. On the site now occupied by the Hilton stood Halfway House, another river-side inn, where Pepys would call in regularly on his walks to and from Deptford and Greenwich. He also used it as a rendezvous, and it was the setting for an episode in May 1663 when he feared he might have been cuckolded:

Thence to the office till the evening, we sat, and then by water (taking Pembleton with us), over the water to the Halfway House, where we played at ninepins, and there my damned jealousy took fire, he and my wife being of a side and I seeing of him take her by the hand in play, though I now believe he did it only in passing and sport.

Pembleton had been employed as a dancing master for Elizabeth; the lessons ceased. On we go.

You'll now be coming up to Surrey Docks Farm. Like all city farms, this is a magical little refuge for people and animals alike. It's also a charity, so I urge you to step inside, make a four-legged friend, and spend lots of money in the farm shop. Then carry on to Greenland Dock, noting its name and the Scandinavian flavour to the names of any number of the streets around you: Queen of Denmark Court, Finland Street, Norway Gate... Note, too, how the character of the buildings has changed, and the size of the dock itself, since this, to me, is one of the few parts of the walk where you can still imagine something of the busy-ness and seriousness of this part of the river as it was in Pepys's day – even though the docks themselves, then known as the Howland Great Wet Dock, were laid out in 1695, after Pepys's retirement. But you still have here the wide quays, the dock-side offices, and above all the comings and goings of boats. Greenland Dock was originally a place for their refitting; then, in the 1720s, its main commercial activity centred on the Greenland whaling ships. By the 1800s, the timber trade had taken over from the whalers, and the docks were the special kingdom of the 'deal porters', who ran the warehouses in which they stored softwood – so-called 'deal' – much of it still coming from the Baltic, in stacks up to eighteen metres high. The deal porters must have been immensely strong and agile men, with a fearless head for heights. In the Second World War, all that timber inevitably made the docks a target for the Luftwaffe who, on the first day of the Blitz, in September 1940, ignited more than a million tons of timber on Quebec Yard, creating the most intense fire ever seen in Britain – surpassing even that of 1666.

Walk just a little further and you will come to a boundary stone designed to horribly confuse the unwary, as it announces you are now on the county border between Kent and Surrey. You are not, of course; rather, you are now leaving Rotherhithe for Deptford, and thus you have a decision to make.

Behind you is the Greenland/Surrey Quays Pier. If you plan on ending this walk at the Greenwich Observatory, you may want to save some time (and shoe-leather) and hop on board a Thames Clipper heading first to Masthouse on the Isle of Dogs and then to Greenwich itself. Or, if you are a purist, you may want to reach Greenwich entirely on foot, through Deptford.

Deptford to Pepys would have meant Trinity House, the administrative department of the Navy Office which, among other things, supervised the nation's lighthouses; and it would also mean the Pett dynasty of shipbuilders, a family as close-knit as the Pepyses. The first Peter Pett, master shipwright, worked in Deptford when Elizabeth I was on the throne; by Pepys's time, there were Petts in charge of the shipbuilding in Limehouse, Wapping, Woolwich, and Chatham in Kent. There were even Petts shipbuilding in the New World. Phineas Pett, paterfamilias, left an autobiography and guided his son's construction of the *Sovereign of the Seas* (or the 'Golden Devil', as she was known to her enemies) for Charles I. But the Peter Pett whom Pepys knew was made a scapegoat for that Dutch raid on the Medway in June 1667, accused of not having made the English fleet safe when he might have done so:

He said he used never a boat till they were all gone but one; and that was to carry away things of great value, and these were his models of ships; which, when the Council, some of them, had said they wished that the Dutch had had them instead of the King's ships, he answered, he did believe the Dutch would have made more advantage of the models than of the ships, and that the King had had greater loss thereby; this they all laughed at. After having heard him for an hour or more, they bid him withdraw. I all this while showing him no respect, but rather against him, for which God forgive me! for I mean no hurt to him, but only find that these Lords are upon their own purgation, and it is necessary I should be so in behalf of the office.

'In behalf of the office'. That's Pepys all over.

Rather more happily, Deptford was also the home of his fellow diarist John Evelyn: 'a most beautiful place', as Pepys describes Evelyn's house in 1665. He particularly admired the gardens, 'which are for variety of evergreens, and hedge of holly, the finest things I ever saw in my life'. Evelyn had created his house, Sayes Court, from the ground up in 1663; a map in the British Library records the house's triple-gabled frontage and, stretching along the river behind it, the navy buildings, including the King's Shipyard, the Great Dock, the Storekeeper's House, water gates, another storehouse, a powder-house (where gunpowder was kept), and the houses of Evelyn's neighbours. John Evelyn was one of those who introduced Pepys to the Royal Society and thus to the minds and conversation of men such as the scientist Robert Hooke. Pepys was elected to the society in February 1665, and on 1 May he spent a day with his fellow Royal Societarians, ending at Sayes Court, and records with delight 'noble discourse all day long'.

In 1665, when the Pepyses – along with the Navy Office and anyone else in the city who possibly could – fled London and the plague, this became Pepys's neighbourhood too, and that of many other acquaintances from his London life: Lord Brouncker and that feisty troublemaker of a mistress of his, Abigail Williams; the noisy and dissipated Captain George Cocke, who was a drinking companion of Pepys, with business interests in the Baltic; and William Sheldon, another naval administrator, with whose family Elizabeth lodged that summer in Woolwich, out near what is now the site of the Thames Barrier. Samuel records one especially merry evening on 10 September 1665, boosted by the news of a naval victory:

> the receipt of this newes did put us all into such an extacy of joy... that in all my life I never met with so merry a two hours as our company this night was. Among other humours, Mr. Evelyn's repeating of some verses made up of nothing but the various acceptations of may and can, and doing it so aptly upon occasion of something of that nature, and so fast, did make us all die almost with laughing... In this humour we sat till about ten at night, and so my Lord and his mistress home, and we to bed, it being one of the times of my life wherein I was the fullest of true sense of joy.

But why did Elizabeth and Sam not lodge together? That's another mystery. He was extraordinarily busy in 1665, with two new appointments as well as all the extra work created by the plague itself; but it may be that Sam so arranged matters simply to give himself a break. If so, he relished it. 'Thus I ended this month,' he writes on 31 July 1665, while friends and colleagues in the City were falling victim to the plague on a daily basis,

> with the greatest joy that ever I did any in my life, because I have spent the greatest part of it with abundance of joy, and honour, and pleasant journeys, and brave entertainments, and without cost of money...

At the end of the year he is marvelling again:

> Thus ends this year, to my great joy, in this manner. I have raised
> my estate from 1300*l*. in this year to 4400*l*.. I have got myself
> greater interest, I think, by my diligence, and my employments
> encreased by that of Treasurer for Tangier, and Surveyour of
> the Victualls. It is true we have gone through great melancholy
> because of the great plague... But now the plague is abated
> almost to nothing, and I have never lived so merrily (besides
> that I never got so much) as I have done this plague time.

Some men have good wars. Pepys had a good plague.

All of which makes it all the more heartbreaking that so much of
Deptford's naval history was annihilated first by the bombing raids
of the Second World War and second by some inexcusably mala-
droit post-war redevelopment. All the prettiness of Rotherhithe or
the prosperity of Greenwich have been lost here. 'Samuel Pepys' is
a down-at-heel housing estate, and Evelyn's Sayes Court a shabby
park, preserving only a sad and ancient mulberry tree.

However, if you carry on as close to the river as you can into
Deptford, passing through Sayes Court Park, down Prince Street
and then left onto Watergate Street, you will eventually find yourself
at a junction, facing a long brick wall on your left, leading down to
the Thames and, to the right, Borthwick Street. On the other side
of that wall is the so-called Master Shipwright's Palace; the present
building dates from 1708, but there were others on this site from at
least the time of Deptford's Tudor dockyard. The Palace has previ-
ously been open to the public for the Open House London weekend
and, if you can get to see the interior, it will give you an excellent
idea of the regard and significance enjoyed by men such as Peter

Pett. And in Borthwick Street, on the evening of 30 May 1593, the playwright Christopher Marlowe met his end, famously stabbed through the eye either in a drunken brawl or, at the other end of the conspiracy scale, murdered on the orders of Sir Francis Walsingham. Walk to the end of Borthwick Street and, if you have time, turn right down Deptford Green to St Nicholas Church, where on its east wall you will find a plaque in Marlowe's memory, and pay your respects. Otherwise, bear left toward Glaisher Street and cross Deptford Creek into Royal Greenwich, but not before noting the statue of Peter the Great, holding court beside the creek itself. And yes, Peter was here in 1698, renting Sayes Court (which he trashed – that holly hedge was never the same again) in order to study the genius of British shipbuilding and take such knowledge back home.

Greenwich gives this walk rather a bravura finish. Although much of its character now comes from the time of Admiral Nelson's navy, there are still places here where we can follow Pepys, the first of which is in Greenwich's heart: St Alfege Church. Turn right, leaving the river behind you, then left along Creek Road (the A200) into Greenwich itself. Follow Greenwich Church Street (the A206) round to the right, and St Alfege will be on your right. Pepys worshipped at St Alfege during his time lodging in Greenwich in 1665, and he records with particular approval being able to sit very near Anne Lethieullier, a London neighbour, whom he describes as 'my fat brown beauty of our Parish'. The present church is one of Hawksmoor's, from 1718, and it is a wonderful clear, clean space with superb acoustics. From Pepys's era, it retains some original carvings by Grinling Gibbons as well as a triple-decker keyboard, parts of which date back to the time of the celebrated musician Thomas Tallis (*c.*1505–1585), and might have been played by him. Henry VIII was baptised here, while the churchyard is the resting place for both Tallis and John Lethieullier, Anne's husband. And it was in a little meeting room in the church that the Greenwich authorities voted on the fate of the child rescued from the plague in Gracechurch Street, whom we met on Walk 2. (She was allowed to stay.)

Then, of course, there is the Old Royal Naval College, the Queen's House and, up the hill in the park, the Royal Observatory. Pepys had connections to all three. Although technically retired by this time, he acted as an advisor (thanks to the good offices of John Evelyn) while the Royal Naval Hospital – now the Old Royal Naval College – was being built in 1694. And he would no doubt have been delighted, if astounded, to find the National Maritime Museum here. We can imagine the landscaping of Greenwich Park would have fascinated him, as did that of St James's Park (see Walk 3), and we know that in 1662 he viewed the Queen's House as it was being done up for Charles II's mother, the Dowager Queen Henrietta Maria. But be warned: this is a long end piece to our walk, and really Greenwich is another stopping-off point that deserves a whole day to explore on its own. If you are ready to call it a day, I suggest that a boat is a suitably maritime way to get back into central London – there is a pier for the Thames River Bus at Greenwich, as well as stations for the DLR.

Or, if you have the energy, end your walk through the grounds of the Old Royal Naval College and Greenwich Park, up to the observatory. To do this, walk from St Alfege back along Greenwich Church Street, then through the splendid gate into College Way and the grounds of the University of Greenwich and of the Old Royal Naval College. If you experience a sense of déjà vu in doing so, that is because the university's grounds have featured in movies from *Les Misérables* to *Thor: The Dark World*. Turn right past the Painted Hall of the Old Royal Naval College – one of the finest Baroque interiors in Europe, and a brother to the Banqueting House on Walk 1. Crossing Romney Road, the National Maritime Museum and the Queen's House are before you. The museum can answer every question you might ever have about the Stuart navy, but again, it should be visited when there is time to appreciate it fully. The Queen's House is a little less time-consuming, and still records how a fashionable apartment of the 1660s would have appeared, complete with the first cantilevered spiral staircase in England. And then – and I admire your stamina, if you do this – push on into Greenwich Park and tackle that hill up to the Royal Observatory. Built at top speed between 1675 and 1676, the Royal Observatory both stands on and created the Greenwich Meridian, from which all lines of longitude and time zones are still determined today, and which arguably gave the British navy the dominance it was to enjoy for 200 years to come. Stand with one foot on either side of the line and think: Samuel Pepys would be proud.

WALK 5

A New Year's Day Walk

THIS FINAL WALK through Pepys's London is planned for that time of year when today's Londoners are most likely to get out and stretch their legs. With a nod to the Diary's beginning, on New Year's Day 1660, it visits places specifically to do with Christmas and the New Year in Pepys's household, as well as a few more of London's surviving seventeenth-century original buildings, or almost originals. It's the shortest walk in the book – a *bonne bouche*, if you like, to end with – although it does have the option to extend it all the way out to Wapping, a part of the riverside that saw Samuel Pepys strolling through it almost as often as Deptford and Greenwich.

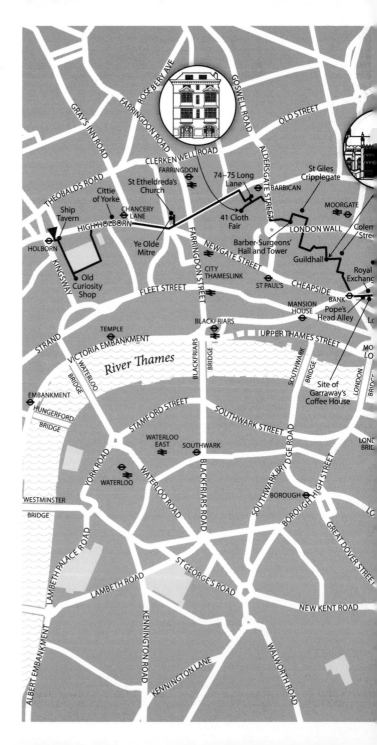

GRAY'S INN ROAD

ROSEBERY AVE

FARRINGDON ROAD

GOSWELL ROAD

OLD STREET

THEOBALDS ROAD

CLERKENWELL ROAD

FARRINGDON

ALDERSGATE STREET

St Giles
Cripplegate

Cittie
of Yorke

St Etheldreda's
Church

74–75 Long
Lane

BARBICAN

MOORGATE

Ship
Tavern

CHANCERY
LANE

HOLBORN

HIGH HOLBORN

41 Cloth
Fair

LONDON WALL

Colem
Stre

HOLBORN

Ye Olde
Mitre

NEWGATE STREET

Barber-Surgeons'
Hall and Tower

Guildhall

KINGSWAY

FARRINGDON STREET

CITY
THAMESLINK

Royal
Exchange

Old
Curiosity
Shop

FLEET STREET

ST PAUL'S

CHEAPSIDE

BANK

MANSION
HOUSE

Pope's
Head Alley

Lo

STRAND

TEMPLE

BLACKFRIARS

UPPER THAMES STREET

MO
LO

VICTORIA EMBANKMENT

BLACKFRIARS

BLACKFRIARS BRIDGE

SOUTHWARK

SOUTHWARK BRIDGE

LONDON BRIDGE

BRIDGE

River Thames

EMBANKMENT

WATERLOO BRIDGE

Site of
Garraway's
Coffee House

HUNGERFORD
BRIDGE

STAMFORD STREET

SOUTHWARK STREET

LONE
BRI

YORK ROAD

WATERLOO
EAST

SOUTHWARK

WATERLOO

WATERLOO ROAD

BLACKFRIARS ROAD

SOUTHWARK BRIDGE ROAD

LO

WESTMINSTER

BOROUGH

BOROUGH HIGH STREET

BRIDGE

GREAT DOVER STREET

LAMBETH PALACE ROAD

LAMBETH ROAD

ST GEORGE'S ROAD

NEW KENT ROAD

ALBERT EMBANKMENT

KENNINGTON ROAD

KENNINGTON LANE

WALWORTH ROAD

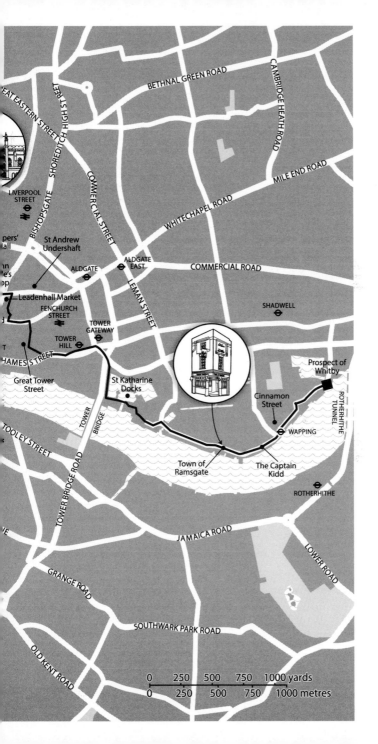

GREAT EASTERN STREET

BETHNAL GREEN ROAD

CAMBRIDGE HEATH ROAD

SHOREDITCH HIGH STREET

BISHOPSGATE

COMMERCIAL STREET

MILE END ROAD

LIVERPOOL STREET

pers' all

St Andrew Undershaft

WHITECHAPEL ROAD

ALDGATE

ALDGATE EAST

COMMERCIAL ROAD

LEMAN STREET

Leadenhall Market

FENCHURCH STREET

SHADWELL

TOWER GATEWAY

TOWER HILL

THAMES STREET

Great Tower Street

St Katharine Docks

Prospect of Whitby

Cinnamon Street

ROTHERHITHE TUNNEL

TOWER BRIDGE

WAPPING

TOOLEY STREET

TOWER BRIDGE ROAD

Town of Ramsgate

The Captain Kidd

ROTHERHITHE

JAMAICA ROAD

LOWER ROAD

GRANGE ROAD

SOUTHWARK PARK ROAD

OLD KENT ROAD

| 0 | 250 | 500 | 750 | 1000 yards |
| 0 | 250 | 500 | 750 | 1000 metres |

New Year's Day is always an excellent day for a London walk. The pavements are emptier, the streets quieter; what Pepys called 'much business' is taking a pause before rolling up its sleeves and plunging into the next twelve months. There's no necessity, by any means, for the walk to take place exactly then but, if you do head out in January, select your footwear with care. Samuel was a great fan of 'a fine frosty morning', but on 9 January 1665 he records the following:

> Up and walked to White Hall, it being still a brave frost, and
> I in perfect good health, blessed be God! In my way saw a
> woman that broke her thigh, in her heels slipping up upon the
> frosty streete.

London's pavements, when icy, are hardly less forgiving now.

Start at Holborn Tube station. Come out onto High Holborn, turn right and, almost at once, turn right again down one of those familiar squeezed alleyways, this one being New Turnstile. Turn left along Gate Street, and there before you is the Ship Tavern, with its proud boast of having been founded in 1549. Some of the pub's claims for its history are perhaps to be taken with a tiny grain of salt, but it's a very pleasing building all the same, and an excellent pub. We will shortly encounter an even more historic building, but first, follow Gate Street down until it becomes Lincoln's Inn Fields and walk along the western edge of this precious green space. We know how frequently Pepys patronised the theatre here and, indeed, here he was on 1 January 1663. He and Elizabeth had been spending the evening with Edward Montagu, Earl of Sandwich, Samuel's most significant patron since his earliest days as a clerk, and he reports that they 'lay long abed', not rising until 10 o'clock (a rare occurrence for Sam), and then enjoyed a lazy morning catching up on all the latest court gossip with Montagu's housekeeper, Sarah – stories that left even Samuel feeling somewhat puritanical: 'I find that there is nothing almost but bawdry at Court from top to bottom,' he wrote. And then he and Elizabeth went off to the Duke's House theatre to see *The Villain* by Thomas Porter (more or less a Restoration reworking of *Othello*). Sam's verdict: 'The more I see it, the more I am offended at my first undervaluing the play, it being very good and pleasant, and yet a true and allowable tragedy'. The performance was enlivened by the fact that the retired actress Hester Davenport, now the mistress of the Earl of Oxford, was in the audience, 'in a velvet gown and very handsome'. Cunningham, in 1850, says that Montagu was living in Lincoln's Inn Fields at this time, very close to the Duke's House theatre, so it had been a very leisurely morning indeed.

You should now be at the southern end of Lincoln's Inn Fields and looking down Portsmouth Street, where a genuine, venerable survivor awaits you in the form of the Old Curiosity Shop. This is alleged to have been the childhood home of Charles Dickens's Little Nell, or at least intended to be so by the author. Whatever the truth of that, the building dates from 1567 and is thought to be the oldest shop in London. Almost a hundred years later, Lord Clare created Clare Market here, and nearby was Gibbon's Tennis Court, which became the first home of Thomas Killigrew's company of actors and actresses (see Walk 3). (The shambles, connected to the market, also contained an area set aside for kosher butchers, intriguingly enough.)

Take an amble from here around Lincoln's Inn Fields' southern and eastern edges, until you come to Great Turnstile, at the top north-east corner. The street's name records a barrier used to stop horses entering. Head down it now, turn right, and carry on down

High Holborn until you reach the Cittie of Yorke pub. The present building dates to the 1920s, but there has been a tavern here since 1430. This is the first of two historic pubs – the second is the Old Mitre, for which you need to continue down High Holborn, turn off into Charterhouse Street, and then into Ely Place. A historic legal oddity means that the ground here is (technically) a part of Cambridge, not London at all, and supposedly the London police can only set foot on it if invited. The Bishop of Ely had his palace here until 1576, when Elizabeth I encouraged him to move and the palace became the home of her chancellor, Sir Christopher Hatton (as in Hatton Garden, to which indeed the garden to his house extended). St Etheldreda's church is right next door and eminently worth exploring. First, the church itself dates from the thirteenth century, with part of the crypt containing even older walls that may be from London's Roman basilica. In 1620, it became a private chapel for the Catholic Spanish Ambassador; in 1642, it was both a prison and a hospital. Like many of the oldest churches, it was very simply planned, but it was strong enough to survive the Blitz, as was its fourteenth-century west window, miraculously enough. It is now one of the oldest Catholic churches in England.

Walk along Charterhouse Street and past Smithfield Market, which you may remember from Walk 2. This time, however, turn right down Lindsey Street and left into Long Lane. You're looking for Number 74–75 which, believe it or not, constitutes a single house that, behind its later façades, dates from 1598 and is another survivor of the Fire. Kinghorn Street, found via a covered passage to the right, leads you down into Cloth Fair. There, turn right and look out for Number 41. This is the oldest house in the City of London, beating that in Long Lane by a single year. It was built between 1597 and 1614 and, yes, it has been somewhat squared up and made tidy, but somehow you still know as you look at it that you are looking at something very old indeed. Pepys might not have recorded a presence here, but Cloth Fair itself was the home to drapers and cloth merchants, Inigo Jones's father among them, and Pepys's father, John the tailor, must have known this street well.

Walk back along Cloth Fair (which becomes Middle Street), heading east, and turn right down Cloth Street to Aldersgate Street. Turn south down Aldersgate Street and then right into the open spaces of the Barbican. You are now outside old London Wall, and we will linger here as briefly as possible, but there are two sights to see. One is Barber-Surgeons' Hall, and beside it the stump of a tower: the hall has been completely rebuilt, albeit on its original site, but the tower is part of the medieval defences along London's city wall and dates back to the thirteenth century. Pepys dined in the original hall at least twice, once on 27 February 1663:

About 11 o'clock, Commissioner Pett and I walked to Chyrurgeon's Hall (we being all invited thither, and promised to dine there); where we were led into the Theatre; and by and by comes the reader, Dr. Tearne, with the Master and Company, in a very handsome manner: and all being settled, he begun his lecture, this being the second upon the kidneys, ureters, &c., which was very fine; and his discourse being ended, we walked into the Hall, and there being great store of company, we had a fine dinner and good learned company, many Doctors of Phisique, and we used with extraordinary great respect.

Among other observables we drank the King's health out of a gilt cup given by King Henry VIII. to this Company, with bells hanging at it, which every man is to ring by shaking after he hath drunk up the whole cup. There is also a very excellent piece [painting] of the King, done by Holbein, stands up in the Hall, with the officers of the Company kneeling to him to receive their Charter.

The Worshipful Company of Barbers still owns both the painting, which dates to 1542, and the 'Grace Cup' with its bells.

And then, more or less opposite, there is St Giles Cripplegate. This, too, is a reconstruction; the Tudor church was destroyed during the Blitz, when pretty much the whole of this part of London was reduced to rubble, from which sprang the hymn to concrete we see today. But the church was worth restoring, if for no other reason than the fact that Oliver Cromwell married Elizabeth Bourchier here on 22 August 1620 and John Milton was buried here in 1674 – and then, in 1790, suffered the indignity of having his grave opened and some of the teeth knocked from his jaw and taken as souvenirs.

Time to come back down into the City proper. Go right to Wood Street, then head south. The solitary little tower in the centre of Wood Street is all that remains, since November 1940, of the church of St Albans; note too, off to your left, Love Lane, 'so called because of wantons', as Stow puts it censoriously. Visitors to London often recorded their amazement at the number of sex workers to be found in just about every area of the City; clearly, this was one of them.

Wood Street itself was where you came to buy or commission furniture and joinery. Pepys often did a deal of household shopping over the Christmas period, and he records his purchases in the Diary (and after all, what would Christmas be without some retail therapy?). He was here in 1663 on 6 January, otherwise known as Twelfth Night (which was usually the biggest celebration of the season, with family gatherings and games and a special Twelfth-Night cake). 'Then into Wood St,' he begins:

and there bought a fine table for my dining-room, cost me
50*s*.... and after dinner to the Duke's house, and there saw
'Twelfth Night' acted well, though it be but a silly play, and not
related at all to the name or day.

It turned out to be an expensive day:

Thence Mr. Battersby the apothecary, his wife, and I and mine
by coach together, and setting him down at his house, he paying
his share, my wife and I home, and found all well, only myself
somewhat vexed at my wife's neglect in leaving of her scarf,
waistcoat, and night-dressings in the coach today that brought
us from Westminster, though, I confess, she did give them to me
to look after, yet it was her fault not to see that I did take them
out of the coach. I believe it might be as good as 25*s*. loss or
thereabouts.

Turn down Love Lane, past the garden of St Mary Aldermanbury,
where in what was the churchyard of this now-vanished church
there lie the bones of Henry Condell and John Heminges – both key
figures in the preservation of the First Folio of Shakespeare's plays
– and, rather less nobly, the 'Hanging Judge', Judge Jeffreys, whom
you will remember from Walk 4. We will hear more of him before
this last walk is done. Turn to your right, and you will be looking at
London's Guildhall. Walk to the centre of its square.

There are three parts to this pale and beautiful London square,
which today, to me, has something of that same bleached elegance
as St Mark's in Venice. First, there is the Guildhall itself, the only
secular stone building to survive from pre-1666. If Westminster
governed the country, then it was from the Guildhall that London

was run. It was begun in 1411; its chapel consecrated in 1444. The lower parts of its walls are certainly pre-Fire, with some additions by Wren after the roof burned off. Pepys is quite fittingly much in evidence here: there is a window dedicated to him in the hall, and his bust is to be found in front of the Guildhall Art Gallery along with that of Dick Whittington and, in front of the Guildhall, those of London's legendary giants: Gog and Magog.

The Guildhall was repaired at speed after the Fire, so important was it deemed in the civic life of London. Accidents among the workmen were frequent: 'I passed by Guildhall, which is almost finished,' Sam notes in May 1669, 'and saw a poor labourer carried by, I think, dead with a fall, as many there are, I hear'. Near neighbour to the Guildhall used to be the Clockmaker's Museum; this has now moved to the Science Museum but allows an excuse here for the story of Sam and his timepieces. He received a gift of a watch from one Timothy Briggs, a scrivener (it may have been a bribe) in May 1665:

> But, Lord! to see how much of my old folly and childishnesse hangs upon me still that I cannot forbear carrying my watch in my hand in the coach all this afternoon, and seeing what o'clock it is one hundred times; and am apt to think with myself, how could I be so long without one; though I remember since, I had one, and found it a trouble, and resolved to carry one no more about me while I lived.

But it was not in his possession long, ending up in September 1666 as a bribe to Lord Brouncker, then a new acquaintance at the Navy Office:

He do now give me a watch, a plain one, in the roome of my former watch with many motions which I did give him. If it goes well, I care not for the difference in worth, though believe there is above 5*l*...

Toys for boys!

The Guildhall also has an art gallery, again not to be missed, with a particularly lovely and unexpected collection of Pre-Raphaelite masterpieces, and – lo and behold – on its lower floor, the remains of London's Roman amphitheatre, marking how this site has always been central to London's history in every way.

Go east out of the Guildhall to Basinghall Street, and head south, then east along Masons Avenue, past a pub with the rather wonderful name of Old Doctor Butler's Head (Doctor Butler was a physician at the court of James I, but the pub is from the nineteenth century), and into Coleman Street. Coleman Street was something of a Puritan stronghold in the years leading up to the Civil War: in 1642, the five MPs Charles I had tried to arrest in the House of Commons hid here, and the Swan tavern once in Coleman Street was reputedly used as a meeting place by Cromwell. There is precious little left above ground here to show it, but this part of London is old as old can be. Come south to Lothbury and, if you care to, indulge in another brief detour: turn left and follow Lothbury until it becomes Throgmorton Street, and detour left up Throgmorton Avenue. Here you will find the Hall of the Drapers' Company, which is itself on the site of Austin Friars, once the home of Thomas Cromwell. Otherwise, turn right from Lothbury down Princes Street to Bank, and then take the second left, down Cornhill. On your right you will pass Pope's Head Alley where, in the Pope's Head tavern (run by John Sawyer, a friend), Pepys first sampled 'a dish of tay' and in the alley bought luxury knick-knacks including tweezers, scissors, and an agate-handled knife. On your left, you will soon come up to one of seventeenth-century London's favourite shopping malls – the Royal Exchange – which sells many such small and unnecessary indulgences today.

Sir Thomas Gresham (*c.*1519–1579; Gresham Street was named after him) put up the first building here, borrowing the idea from Antwerp. Just as now, it was an open-galleried four-sided arcade of shops, which sadly proved its undoing during the Fire, when the flames ran round the galleries and down the stairs unhindered. The present building, still following the spirit of the old plan, was opened in 1844. The creature on its weathervane is the golden grass-hopper from Gresham's family crest – not one of the dead insectoid Martians from the 1967 London horror film *Quatermass and the Pit*, as you might have been forgiven for thinking. In the 1660s, this was not only a retail centre but a place to meet with colleagues, to catch up on news and gossip, and to refuel for the rest of the working day. And, if you were Samuel Pepys (and if you came without your wife), to flirt with the prettiest of the shopkeepers. 'I to the Exchange', he writes on 20 December 1665:

> to see whether my pretty seamstress be come again or no, and I find she is, so I to her, saluted her over her counter [that is, snatched a kiss] in the open Exchange above, and mightily joyed to see her, poor pretty woman! I must confess I think her a great beauty.

When they shopped together, Samuel and Elizabeth tended to pat-ronise the New Exchange in the Strand. It was there, on 2 January 1668, that Sam purchased £3 of lace for a handkerchief as a New

Year's gift for Elizabeth, while his assistant Will Hewer – who had something of a pash on his employer's wife – presented her with a diamond locket worth more than ten times as much. January the following year 1669 saw Sam and Will shopping together:

> he and I to the cabinet-shops, to look out, and did agree, for a
> cabinet to give my wife for a New-year's gift; and I did buy one
> cost me 11*l.*, which is very pretty, of walnutt-tree.

Lesson learned. The whole business of Christmas presents was clearly just as fraught then as now.

One of the charming but little appreciated characteristics of this part of London is the number of narrow alleys connecting the main thoroughfares, something like the famous 'Passages Couverts' in Paris. If you were to wander down Change Alley for example (site of Garraway's Coffee House, which opened in 1658 and was still going strong in Dickens's day), you will find yourself on Lombard Street. This was the Little Italy of Restoration London – full of Italian merchants and bankers – and Christmas Eve 1660 saw Pepys here at the goldsmith's shop run by alderman Edward Backwell. Sam was hurriedly buying a pair of silver candlesticks as a Christmas gift for Sir William Coventry – his friend Peter Pett, whom we met on Walk 4, having quietly clued Sam in to the fact that this was the done thing. (It is so Pepysian that not only the gift but the choice of person to buy it from was done with such professional awareness.) Then home:

> and with the painters till 10 at night, making an end of my
> house and the arch before my door, and so this night I was rid of
> them and all other work, and my house was made ready against
> to-morrow being Christmas day.

The first Christmas in Seething Lane. But we digress. Come back to Cornhill, leaving the Exchange behind you, and walk east past Finch Lane (and somewhere here, Pepys's print-seller John Cade had his shop – after the Fire, he relocated to a spot now under the foundations of the 183-metre-tall Tower 42), past Newman's Court (which may be where Dickens imagined Scrooge's counting house), past St Peter-upon-Cornhill, and into Leadenhall Street, where Pepys saw morris dancers in May 1663. We're now in the parish of St Andrew Undershaft, where Pepys's Uncle Wight's house was to be found near the church. The church's unusual name seems to have come from the fact that a maypole was set up outside it annually until 1517, when a riot made the church authorities feel such jollification might be unwise; a maypole would have been of a piece with Pepys's sudden discovery close by of those morris-men, in the middle of a City street, as another part of some ancient May-time tradition.

Uncle Wight was wealthy, and Pepys had hopes of being made his heir, so Uncle Wight enjoyed a good deal of Samuel's hospitality and wasn't shy of demanding his company either – which both Samuel and Elizabeth found onerous. New Year 1664 saw Samuel present Uncle Wight with a swan for roasting, but, although they saw it on his table, made into a pie, when they joined him for dinner on New Year's Day, they didn't get to sample it (rather like those dinner parties where the good bottle of wine you contributed never makes an appearance), and they had to make excuses to get away to the King's House to see *Henry VIII*. Samuel finally got to try some of the swan pie on 10 January – by which time it must have been long past its best – and then felt he had to invite the Wights for a proper roast swan later that week. Elizabeth was livid. Nonetheless she set to, and on 12 January:

> We [the Pepyses and Uncle and Aunt Wight] had a good
> dinner, the chief dish a swan roasted, and that excellent meate.
> At, dinner and all day very merry. After dinner to cards, where
> till evening, then to the office a little, and to cards again with
> them, and lost half-a-crowne. They being gone, my wife did tell
> me how my uncle did this day accost her alone, and spoke of his
> hoping she was with child, and kissing her earnestly told her he
> should be very glad of it, and from all circumstances methinks
> he do seem to have some intention of good to us, which I shall
> endeavour to continue more than ever I did yet.

I applaud Elizabeth's forbearance of her husband and his nosey rela-
tives, both.

And so, turning right, we come to Leadenhall Market, today one
of those airy Victorian cast-iron arcades. Pass straight through the
market, and you'll emerge on Lime Street; turning right, left, and
later right again will take you onto Mincing Lane via Fenchurch
Street, and at the end of Mincing Lane you should turn left onto
Great Tower Street. On the corner ahead of you there is a pub now
called the Hung, Drawn and Quartered, once the site of one of
Pepys's favourite locals, the Dolphin, where Will Hewer (the young
scamp!) got outrageously drunk on Twelfth Night in 1662 in his
master's absence:

> I hear that my man Gull [Pepys is either too amused or too
> angry to fuss about spellings] was gone to bed, and upon
> enquiry I hear that he did vomit before he went to bed, and
> complained his head ached, and thereupon though he was
> asleep I sent for him out of his bed, and he rose and came up
> to me, and I appeared very angry and did tax him with being

drunk, and he told me that he had been with Mr. Southerne and Homewood at the Dolphin, and drank a quart of sack...

Sack was a Spanish wine, sweetened and mixed with spices and sometimes served warm. It's best not to contemplate the kind of hangover that could give you.

Carry on along Great Tower Street to Byward Street, then, turning left, to the Tower of London itself via Tower Hill. On the very early morning of Christmas Eve 1664, Pepys was here, stargazing:

> Having sat up all night to past two o'clock this morning, our
> porter, being appointed, comes and tells us that the bellman
> tells him that the star is seen upon Tower Hill; so I, that had
> been all night setting in order all my old papers in my chamber,
> did leave off all, and my boy and I to Tower Hill, it being a
> most fine, bright moonshine night, and a great frost; but no
> Comet to be seen.

He finally caught sight of it on the evening of the same day:

> This evening I being informed did look and saw the Comet,
> which is now, whether worn away or no I know not, but appears
> not with a tail, but only is larger and duller than any other star,
> and is come to rise betimes, and to make a great arch, and is
> gone quite to a new place in the heavens than it was before.

The comet, often referred to simply as 'the great comet of 1664', is now known as C/1664 W1. (I wish they would rename it after Pepys.)

Elizabeth spent the Christmas of 1664 inside nursing a black eye, to Sam's great demerit, and with Sam making endless excuses for her nonappearance and upbraiding himself *as well he might* for the 'passion' in which he had struck her. But as the old year turned to the new, they seem to have mended matters between them.

Soon as ever the clock struck one, I kissed my wife in the kitchen by the Fireside, wishing her a merry new yeare, observing that I believe I was the first proper wisher of it this year, for I did it as soon as ever the clock struck one. So ends the old yeare, I bless God, with great joy to me... and a pretty and loving quiett family I have as any man in England.

Perhaps he had that last Christmas ruefully in mind when he wrote on Christmas Day 1665:

To church in the morning, and there saw a wedding in the church, which I have not seen many a day; and the young people so merry one with another, and strange to see what delight we married people have to see these poor fools decoyed into our condition, every man and woman gazing and smiling at them.

But not all Christmases were like that. Twelfth Night 1669, which was to be the last that Samuel and Elizabeth enjoyed together, was a far merrier occasion:

At noon comes Mrs. Turner and Dyke, and Mrs. Dickenson, and then comes The. and Betty Turner, the latter of which is a very pretty girl; and then Creed and his wife, whom I sent for, by my coach. These were my guests, and Mrs. Turner's friend, whom I saw the other day, Mr. Wicken, and very merry we were at dinner, and so all the afternoon, talking, and looking up and down my house; and in the evening I did bring out my cake – a noble cake, and there cut it into pieces, with wine and good drink: and after a new fashion, to prevent spoiling the cake, did put so many titles into a hat, and so drew cuts; and I was the Queene; and The. Turner, King – Creed, Sir Martin Marr-all; and Betty, Mrs. Millicent: and so we were mighty merry till it was night; and then, being moonshine and fine frost, they went home, I lending some of them my coach to help to carry them, and so my wife and I spent the rest of the evening in talk and reading, and so with great pleasure to bed.

And we could do worse than leave them there, too.

But if you wish to continue walking, work your way with care around the tangle of junctions and traffic lights round Tower Hill, and pick up St Katharine's Way, which will take you round St Katharine Docks to Wapping High Street. In Pepys's day there were timber yards and rope works all the way along the river here, and Samuel also came here for a naval funeral, of Robert Blake, in April 1661. The greatest of the timber merchants, Sir William Warren, had a yard here in Wapping as well as one in Rotherhithe (the Wapping yard was just about where Cinnamon Street is today, behind the Overground station). Pepys thought highly of Sir William – 'a most able and worthy man,' he calls him in December 1663:

and understanding seven times more than ever I thought to be in him... and did give me a common but a most excellent saying to observe in all my life. He did give it in rhyme, but the sense was this, that a man should treat every friend in his discourse and opening his mind to him as of one that may hereafter be his foe.

How wisest of all to open one's mind in a Diary, instead.

Many a sailor had his home here in Wapping, too, and when in June 1667 fear of the Dutch was at a height and discontent among the navy at its worst, Wapping was a flashpoint:

> the hearts as well as affections of the seamen are turned away; and in the open streets in Wapping, and up and down, the wives have cried publickly, 'This comes of your not paying our husbands; and now your work is undone, or done by hands that understand it not.' And Sir W. Batten told me that he was himself affronted with a woman, in language of this kind, on Tower Hill publickly yesterday; and we are fain to bear it, and to keep one at the office door to let no idle people in, for fear of firing of the office and doing us mischief.

Unsurprisingly, where there were sailors, there were sailors' taverns. The first you will encounter today is the Town of Ramsgate, so named as this was where the fishermen of Ramsgate used to land their catch. The mock gallows outside the pub are where we catch up with Judge Jeffreys again. The Glorious Revolution of 1688 – which saw the Catholic King James II go into exile and his Protestant daughter Mary and her husband William come over from Holland to take James's place upon the throne, and which saw Samuel Pepys resign his offices and retire – marked the end for Judge Jeffreys too. Despite having shaved off those savage eyebrows in an attempt at disguising himself, he was recognised by a man who had come up against him on the bench and who swore he could never forget Jeffreys' face. Taken prisoner at this very pub, he narrowly escaped being torn apart by the mob. Instead he was thrown into the Tower, where he very shortly died. A bad end to a very bad soul. Execution

Dock, where Jeffreys is supposed to have watched so many of his victims suffer (see Walk 4), and where the bodies of those executed had to hang until three tides had passed over them, is probably also roughly where the current Overground station is to be found, but no one is entirely sure. Perhaps the place is best forgotten.

One of those who died there was the pirate Captain William Kidd (*c.*1655–1701), after whom the next riverside pub is named (although it has only been a pub since the 1980s); and then finally we come to the Prospect of Whitby, which vies with the Town of Ramsgate in the drama of Jeffreys' arrest – supposedly he was spotted in the one and chased along the riverbank to the other. What is certain is that there has been a pub here since 1520, when the place was full of seafarers and dedicated to their wants. It claims Pepys among its patrons, along with Dickens and the painters Turner and Whistler. It's an excellent place to pause and think out of time for a moment. For who can watch a river flow and not think of the passage of history – and who can think of the history of London and not think of Samuel Pepys?

Acknowledgements

WRITING A BOOK of walks during lockdown makes one appreciate as never before the wealth of knowledge and information available online. In particular, I have to single out the quite wonderful website pepysdiary.com, created and run by Phil Gyford and augmented and embellished over the years by a host of Pepys enthusiasts. It is everything a website could or should be – intuitive, lively, constantly improved – and was absolutely invaluable in creating this book. I cannot recommend it too highly. It also includes three walks of its own, created by Glyn Thomas, which were inspirational to me in creating the five in this book, and which I returned to as touchstones over and over again.

Every bit as valuable and fascinating is the website layers-oflondon.org, which reproduces in brilliantly zoom-able detail an essential selection of maps recording London's history and growth, and which enabled me to fly like a present-day drone over the streets and squares and alleys and great buildings of the London of Samuel Pepys's day, both before and after the Great Fire.

I must as always record my gratitude to the staff of the British Library, who in the extraordinary circumstances of 2020 maintained as ever their haven for the mind, even if it had to be online, and then as the final draft of this book was coming into being, were able to briefly welcome all us writers and researchers back into their reading rooms. It was a lovely moment to be there again. I was also given generous assistance by Huong Hoang of St Olave Hart Street, and by Fiona Healey-Hutchinson and Barnaby Bryan of Middle Temple, and by Suzie Jenvey of St Alfege, Greenwich.

I must also thank my intrepid fellow walkers, as the five routes detailed here were tested on the ground: Barbara Schwepcke, Lee Ripley, and Mark Polizzotti. It was a unique and uniquely strange experience to be able to nip back and forth over London's streets during lockdown without even a thought to the traffic, but it did mean, sadly, that for one or two of the locations described here I had to rely on research and memory. It goes without saying that any errors in their description are thus doubly mine. If you should find one, gentle reader, please let us know. And to my agent, Chelsey Fox, and to all the staff at Haus Publishing, especially Harry Hall, my indefatigable and splendid editor Alice Horne, and our sharp-eyed proofreader, Jo Stimfield, special thanks indeed.

Lastly, any writer writing on seventeenth-century London really does have to thank Samuel Pepys himself. The creation of his Diary was the creation of our history, as well as immortalising the city he knew so well. As I walked in his footsteps, I came to realise how he loved it too.

Bibliography

FOR SAMUEL PEPYS'S DIARY, pepysdiary.com was the source for all the extracts cited here and for vast amounts of information and detail besides. There are also wonderful and unexpected nuggets of London lore on the londonist.com and the IanVisits blog. I heartily recommend all three.

For Pepys himself, Claire Tomalin's biography *Samuel Pepys: The Unequalled Self* was both guide and inspiration. Liza Picard's *Restoration London* and Stephen Porter's *Pepys's London: Everyday Life in London 1650–1703* were my companions round the city as Pepys would have experienced it. The former does a miraculous job of recreating London from the pavement up; the latter covers a longer period, historically, and has a particularly useful selection of illustrations.

Peter Ackroyd's *London: The Biography* and *The London Encyclopedia* edited by Ben Weinreb, Christopher Hibbert, and John and Julia Keay are bibles, both for style and for reference. Other invaluable sources include Adrian Tinniswood's *By Permission of Heaven: The Story of the Great Fire of London* and Hazel Forsyth's *Butcher, Baker, Candlestick Maker: Surviving the Great Fire of London*; as were Peter Whitfield's *London: A Life in Maps* and Felix Barker and Peter Jackson's *A History of London in Maps*. There is also much to be mined and relished in Christopher Winn's

I Never Knew That About the Thames and in Robert Latham's *The Illustrated Pepys*.

I found myself turning again and again to John Stow's *The Survey of London*, in the second edition with an introduction by Valerie Pearl; to John L. McMullan's *The Canting Crew: London's Criminal Underworld 1550–1700*; and to two essential works from the nineteenth century: Peter Cunningham's enchanting *Handbook of London Past and Present*, of 1850, and Charles Dickens the Younger's *London Guide* of 1879. Both had access to a London far closer to the city Pepys knew than we have now, and shared the sort of obsessive passion for the city that makes a writer today weep tears of gratitude. I also recommend E. V. Lucas's 1909 *A Wanderer in London*. Lucas was writing as the London Pepys knew was being subsumed into that more familiar to us today. *Mayhew's London*, as edited by Peter Quennell, also deals with the nineteenth-century city, but the more you research London's past, the more you realise how it is never wholly gone.

For those of you who become as wholly hooked on Pepys as I am, I recommend Margaret Willes's *The Curious World of Samuel Pepys and John Evelyn*, Ian Mortimer's *The Time Traveller's Guide to Restoration Britain: Life in the Age of Samuel Pepys, Isaac Newton and The Great Fire of London*, Daniel Defoe's *A Journal of the Plague Year*, Phineas Pett's autobiography, as edited by William Gordon Perrin (short, grouchy, self-serving, but with the unmistakable voice of the seventeenth-century navy man), and Arthur Bryant's trilogy on Pepys: *The Man in the Making, The Years of Peril*, and *The Saviour of the Navy*; however old-fashioned their analysis may be in some places, these were the books that for me put Pepys on the map.

Index

A

Aldersgate 45, 58
Apothecaries' Hall 49
Aubrey, John 10, 85
Axe Yard 9–10, 23, 26

B

Backwell, Edward 136
Bagwell, Mrs 13, 55
Banqueting House 17, 27, 122
Barber-Surgeons' Hall 130
Barbican, the 58, 130
Bartholomew Fair 56–7, 77
Batten, Sir William 35, 83, 103, 142
Battersby, John 49, 132
Bedford family, the 30, 81
Bell Yard 35–6, 85
Betjeman, John 66
Bishops of Winchester, the 87, 91
Bloody Mary 56

Borough Market 87, 92
Brouncker, Lord 13, 67, 82–3, 111, 117, 133

C

Cade, John 137
Cambridge 9, 11, 39, 76, 84, 129
Carteret, Sir George and Lady 113
Caxton, William 25, 50
Charles I 11, 22, 27–8, 32, 76, 88, 116, 134
Charles II 11, 22, 25–7, 53, 74–8, 81, 121
Chaucer, Geoffrey 87, 92
Cheapside 40, 52, 60, 62, 84
Cheapside Hoard, the 60
Church of St Bartholomew the Great 52, 57
Civil War, *see* English Civil War

Clapham Common 30
Clifford's Inn 38–9
Clink, the 87, 91
Coleman Street 134
Conan Doyle, Sir Arthur 42
Covent Garden 4, 7, 30, 69,
    80–1, 83, 85
Coventry, Sir William 74, 136
Creed, John 75, 80, 140–1
Cresswell, Elizabeth 88
Cromwell, Oliver 8–11, 21–2,
    25, 32, 35, 80, 131, 134
Cromwell, Richard 10
Cromwell, Thomas 134
Cuckold's Point 112–14

D
Davenport, Hester 128
Davis, Moll 77
Deptford 3, 5, 13, 113–14,
    116–17, 119–20, 123
Dickens, Charles 40, 42, 62,
    65–6, 93–4, 104–5, 128,
    136–7, 143
Donne, John 36
Downing Street 23, 26–7
Downing, George 9, 27, 39
Dryden, John 80–1, 84
Duke of Buckingham 25, 29,
    88

Duke of York, James 73, 75,
    89, 100, 103
Duke's House, the (playhouse)
    73, 77, 85, 128, 132

E
Edward II 53
Edward III 107
Edward VI 24, 53
Elizabeth I 116, 129
Embankment, the Victoria *see*
    Victoria Embankment
English Civil War 9, 21, 34,
    134
Evelyn, John 10, 29–30,
    117–19, 121
Execution Dock 108, 142–3

F
Faithorne and Newcourt map
    4, 79, 81, 85, 104
Feilding, Christopher 58,
    68
Feilding, George, Earl of
    Desmond 54, 68
Fielding, Henry 54
fire, *see* Great Fire, the
Fleet Street 1, 3–4, 11, 17,
    35–42, 51, 75, 79, 86

G

Gibbons, Grinling 78, 120

Globe Theatre, the 86–7, 89

Glorious Revolution of 1688, the 142

Gog and Magog 37, 133

Golden Boy of Pye Corner, the 55

Gordon Riots, the 91

Gower, John 92

Great Fire of 1666
buildings lost 8, 42, 49–50, 52, 55, 60–1, 99, 135
effect on London 3–4, 133, 137
in the diary 2, 12, 33, 51, 91, 100–2, 129
surviving buildings 34–7, 57, 66
see also Monument, the

Great Plague, the 12, 15, 33, 60, 65, 67, 113, 117, 121
in the diary 63–4, 118–19

Greenland Dock 115

Greenwich 3–4, 15, 26, 30, 64–5, 68, 95, 102, 106, 110, 114, 116, 119–23, 146

Gresham, Sir Thomas 135

Guildhall, the 45, 132–4

Gwyn, Nell 25, 31, 76–7, 82

H

Hall, Jacob 60, 87

Harrison, Major-General 28

Henrietta Maria, Queen 32, 76, 121

Henry I 57

Henry VIII 25, 49, 66, 75, 120, 130

Hewer, Will 30, 33, 41, 55, 64, 106, 136, 138

Hinchingbrooke 9, 12

Hogarth, William 14, 80, 84, 112

Holland, Bess 87

Holland, Captain Philip 41

Holland's Leaguer 87–8

Hooke, Robert 117

Hosier Lane 55–6

Houses of Parliament, the 21–2

Huntingdon 9

I

Inns of Court 17, 40

Isabella, the 'She-Wolf of France' 53

Isle of Dogs 3–4, 111, 113–14, 116

J

Jacob's Island 104–5
Jamaica House 106
Jamaica Wine House 62
James I 27, 32, 88, 134
James II 77, 142
Jeffreys, Judge, the 'Hanging Judge' 108, 132, 142–3
Jermyn, Henry, 1st Earl of St Albans 76–7
Johnson, Dr 33–4, 41–2, 84
Jones, Captain Christopher 109–10
Jones, Inigo 17, 27, 30, 32, 39, 81, 130
Jonson, Ben 37

K

Katherine of Aragon 25
Kidd, Captain William 143
Killigrew, Thomas 81, 128
King's House theatre, the 73, 81–2, 137
Knepp, Mrs Elizabeth 13, 35, 81–2
Knights Templar 40, 86

L

Lee Boo, Prince of Palau 109
Leicester Square 79–80

Lilly, William 33
Lincoln's Inn Fields 4, 7, 39–40, 69, 73, 77, 85–6, 88–9, 127–8
Little Ice Age, the 6, 100
London Bridge 5–6, 87, 92, 99, 101–3, 112

M

Mall, the 75
Marlowe, Christopher 120
Martin, Betty 13, 22, 24, 55
Marvell, Andrew 31
Mary I *see* Bloody Mary
Master Shipwright's Palace 119
Mennes, Sir John 35
Mercer, Mary 106
Merchant Taylors' Hall 62
Middle Temple 38, 69, 86
Milton, John 25, 38, 57, 131
Mincing Lane 65–6, 138
Montagu, Edward (1st Earl of Sandwich) 8–9, 11, 25, 127–8
Montagu, Sir Sidney 8
Monument, the 99, 102
More, Sir Thomas 22, 40
Morland, Samuel 11

N

New Exchange, the 30, 135

Newgate Market 7
Newgate Prison 54

O

Olaf II 99, 102
Old Bailey 58
Old Curiosity Shop, the 128

P

Page, Damaris 89, 94
Palace of Whitehall *see*
   Whitehall Palace
Pall Mall 4, 75–6
Penn, Sir William 66, 85, 89
Pepys, Elizabeth 9–10, 12–13,
   17, 23, 28, 35, 45, 51, 55–6, 65,
   67, 77, 81, 85, 101, 106–7, 115,
   118, 127–8, 135–40
Pepys, John 8, 11, 42, 65, 130
Peter the Great 30, 68, 120
Pett, Commissioner Peter 116,
   119–20, 130, 136
Pett, Phineas 116
Piccadilly 4, 78
Pope, Alexander 84
Povey, Thomas 75, 85
Prior, Matthew 80
Protectorate, the 9, 11, 22, 24,
   62

Q

Queen's House, the 121–2

R

Rahere 57
raid on the Medway 102,
   116
Raleigh, Sir Walter 25
Restoration, the 11, 26–7, 39,
   73, 80, 82, 128, 136
Richard II 22
Rotherhithe 107–13, 116, 119,
   141
Royal Observatory, the 95,
   116, 121–2
Royal Society, the 29–30, 32,
   63, 117
Royal Wardrobe, the 50

S

Salisbury Court 1, 17, 42, 73,
   88
Salter, Ada 107
Salter, Dr 107
Sayes Court 117, 119–20
Seething Lane 2, 12, 36, 45,
   65–8, 95, 99, 137
Seymour, Edward, 1st Duke of
   Somerset 24
Shad Thames 104–5

Shakespeare, William 38, 50, 86, 89, 92, 132

Skinner, Mary 13

Smith, Captain John 55, 61

Smithfield 4, 45, 51, 56, 66, 77

Smithfield Market 55–6, 113, 129

Somerset House 24, 30, 32

Southwark 61, 69, 86–7, 91–3, 95, 99, 101, 103

St Bartholomew's Fair, *see* Bartholomew Fair

St Bartholomew's Hospital 53, 55

St Dunstan-in-the-West 36–7

St James's Palace 4, 27, 75

St James's Park 25–7, 69, 74–5, 121

St Olave's Church 24, 66–7

St Paul's Cathedral 4, 45, 52, 61

St Paul's Church 50–1, 83

Staple Inn 40, 60

Stationers' Hall 50–1

Stow, John 24, 52, 57, 88, 93, 99–100, 104, 131

Strand, the 4–5, 28–35, 37, 51, 83, 135

Swift, Jonathan 84, 110

T

Taylor, John 112

Temeraire, HMS 109–10

Temple Bar Gate 35, 51

Temple Church 38, 40, 86

Thames, the 1, 3–5, 23, 60, 86, 90–1, 100, 102–3, 105–6, 108, 111, 119

in the diary 92

Thurloe, John 11

Tonson, Jacob 38

Tower of London, the 3, 26, 66, 79, 139, 142

Trinity House 116

Tsar Peter the Great *see* Peter the Great

Turner, J. M. W. 31, 109–10, 143

Tyburn 54, 56, 83

Tyler, Wat 56

Tyndale, William 36

U

Uncle Wight (Pepys's uncle) 137–8

V

Victoria Embankment, the 29, 86

Villiers, Barbara 25, 78, 89

W

Wallace, William 56

Walton, Izaak 36

Wapping 38, 45, 68, 106–8, 116, 123, 141–2

Westminster 3–4, 13, 17, 23, 28, 75, 102, 132

  Westminster Abbey 23

  Westminster Hall 21–4, 56, 86

Whistler, James McNeill 106, 108, 143

Whitehall 2–4, 9–10, 13, 17, 21–3, 28, 75, 100–1

Whitehall Palace 7, 23, 27, 74

Whittington's Palace 66

Willet, Deb 13, 38, 55

Williams, Abigail 13, 67–8, 82–3, 117

Wilson, Captain Henry 109

Winchester Palace 91

Woolwich 65, 103, 116, 118

Worde, Wynkyn de 42, 50

Worshipful Company of Clothworkers, the 65

Wotton, William 41

Wren, Sir Christopher 34, 42, 52, 60–1, 78, 99, 133

Y

York House 29–30

Digital Walking Routes

Scan the QR code to access the maps in this book in a digital format.